Curriculum Overload

A WAY FORWARD

OECD

BETTER POLICIES FOR BETTER LIVES

This work is published under the responsibility of the Secretary-General of the OECD. The opinions expressed and arguments employed herein do not necessarily reflect the official views of OECD member countries.

This document, as well as any data and map included herein, are without prejudice to the status of or sovereignty over any territory, to the delimitation of international frontiers and boundaries and to the name of any territory, city or area.

The statistical data for Israel are supplied by and under the responsibility of the relevant Israeli authorities. The use of such data by the OECD is without prejudice to the status of the Golan Heights, East Jerusalem and Israeli settlements in the West Bank under the terms of international law.

Note by Turkey
The information in this document with reference to "Cyprus" relates to the southern part of the Island. There is no single authority representing both Turkish and Greek Cypriot people on the Island. Turkey recognises the Turkish Republic of Northern Cyprus (TRNC). Until a lasting and equitable solution is found within the context of the United Nations, Turkey shall preserve its position concerning the "Cyprus issue".

Note by all the European Union Member States of the OECD and the European Union
The Republic of Cyprus is recognised by all members of the United Nations with the exception of Turkey. The information in this document relates to the area under the effective control of the Government of the Republic of Cyprus.

Please cite this publication as:
OECD (2020), *Curriculum Overload: A Way Forward*, OECD Publishing, Paris, *https://doi.org/10.1787/3081ceca-en*.

ISBN 978-92-64-91702-6 (print)
ISBN 978-92-64-81970-2 (pdf)
ISBN 978-92-64-80896-6 (HTML)
ISBN 978-92-64-32326-1 (epub)

Revised version, December 2021
Details of revisions available at: *https://www.oecd.org/about/publishing/Corrigendum-Curriculum-Overload.pdf*

Table of Contents

BOXES

FIGURES

TABLES

Executive Summary

The rapidly changing world places new demands on society and especially the education sector. Skills, attitudes, values, and knowledge about topics such as digital and data literacy, globalisation, literacy for sustainable development, and computational thinking are ever more relevant. Interest groups, parents, teachers, school leaders, and governments may put pressure on the curriculum to change in response to these novel demands. At the same time, curriculum lacks the space to easily add new content without causing overcrowding in the curriculum. Students need to learn deeper and not more; their learning time should not be extended nor should students learn at a surface level. Countries face a significant challenge of being responsive to changing needs while also minimising curriculum expansion and overload.

Curriculum expansion is the tendency to include new content items in a curriculum in response to new societal demands without appropriate adjustment of other parts of the curriculum. Curriculum expansion can result in curriculum overload, which can include: content overload, perceived overload, or curriculum imbalance. Content overload is the excessive amount of content taught in relation to the available time for instruction. Curriculum imbalance occurs when some subjects are given priority at the expense of other areas of the curriculum. Therefore, it is important to address curriculum overload without losing the balance when adding/removing contents.

Perceived overload is the perception on the part of teachers or students of an overcrowded curriculum and can be the result of the perception created by the number of topics and allotted time, assessment periodicity, the size of the curriculum documents and related materials, or lack of readiness to implement new reforms. The perceived or experienced dimensions of curriculum overload are just as important as its actual dimensions, as they can equally undermine the success of a curriculum reform through the loss of support from school leaders, teachers and students.

Student and teacher well-being should be of primary importance in curriculum design, especially when it comes to curriculum overload, because well-being enhances learning, and vice versa. An overloaded curriculum can put pressure on teachers to teach all the material, potentially risking a 'mile-wide, inch-deep' content coverage. Students also may feel stress and pressure, while lacking the time in or out of school to complete all required assignments. This stress, in turn, can undermine students' ability to engage in deeper learning or the productivity or quality of learning time may be lower.

A balance between aiming high and focusing on essentials must be struck so as not to disengage high-performing students or confuse and alienate lower-achieving students. All students need the opportunity to learn and to succeed, no matter their background or skills. As a way of promoting learning for diverse students in different contents, subjects should not be independent blocks, but rather inter-dependent pieces of a puzzle to enable student learning.

The OECD Future of Education and Skills 2030 policy analyses of country/jurisdiction curriculum and reform suggest a variety of approaches to balancing content and competencies to address new societal demands while not overloading the curriculum. For example, countries can embed cross-curricular themes or competencies into existing subjects or structure their curriculum around subject-specific goals. Themes most frequently articulated across countries include "environmental education, sustainability", "local and global citizenship, peace", and "health education, well-being and lifestyle" and are addressed in different subjects depending on the country. Some countries choose to embed them most in the national language whereas others embed them in humanities. Themes themselves may be standalone courses as well.

Countries also may choose to embed cross-curricular competencies in the curriculum. Common cross-curricular competencies include: local and global citizenship, taking responsibility, co-operation ad collaboration, reconciling tensions and dilemmas, creating new value, data literacy, and financial literacy. Cross-curricular competencies can, in turn, be embedded in the curriculum in a variety of ways. As with cross-curricular themes, cross-curricular competencies can be integrated in a variety of subject areas to varying degrees. Subject-specific goals can provide coherence and guidance to school leaders and teachers when they are designed well. Clarity regarding curriculum changes, which often occurs via subject-specific goals, is critical to ensure that teachers have appropriate guidance on how to incorporate new cross-curricular themes and competencies in responding to changing societal demands.

The following are other potential strategies for tackling and mitigating curriculum overload during a redesign process:

- Regulating learning time to avoid the expansion of a curriculum to be an expansion of required learning time.

- Carefully defining the pitch of what is included in curriculum. Balance aiming high while focusing on essentials.

- Build in coherent learning progressions across grades and education levels.

- Focus on conceptual understanding or "big ideas" to avoid an excessive number of subjects or topics within the allotted time.

- Manage perceptions of overload by adjusting the size and/or format of curriculum documents.

Countries have learned a variety of lessons from unintended consequences of curriculum reform to adjust to new curricular demands. Five key lessons identified from country examples include the following:

- Keep the right balance between breadth of learning areas and depth of content knowledge.

- Use focus, rigor, and coherence jointly as key design principles when addressing curriculum overload.

- Be conscious of and avoid homework overload for students.

- Be mindful of local decisions leading to curriculum overload for schools.

- Stress curriculum overload as a pressing issue by redefining student success and well-being.

Curriculum overload can be a stressor to students and teachers and even serve as an impediment to learning. Analyses suggest methods for embedding subjects or competencies and ways to set subject-specific goals. Examples from countries serve as lessons learned or potential strategies that can be adapted to avoid curriculum overload. An effective design process, with a focus on student needs and adoption of effective design strategies can serve as potent examples for countries undergoing curriculum redesign.

Key Messages

Recent societal, technological and economic changes have placed pressure on school systems to adapt their curriculum by including various competencies (e.g. **digital and data literacies, global competencies, financial literacy, media literacy, coding and programming, entrepreneurship, environmental literacy, health literacy, and social and emotional skills**).

However, teaching time over the last decade has not changed much. This creates tensions and competing demands for students to stretch themselves too thinly and not having time for deeper learning; for teachers to embed these competencies within limited instruction time; and for policy makers to resist accommodating all these demands by adding more hours to curriculum. Most importantly, school systems need to be aware that "**more learning time does not necessarily lead to productive student outcomes**", therefore more countries and schools have increasingly become aware of the importance of focusing on **quality of learning time (rather than quantity per se)** as well as **student well-being**. Addressing curriculum overload is also actioned to ensure **teacher well-being** and support **effective teaching**.

To make this curriculum paradigm shift a reality, countries and schools are called to rethink what to change on the scope and structure, what to prioritise/remove among topics without compromising rigour, how to manage change process, etc. For example, they are making changes such as regulating the quantity and **ensuring the quality of learning time**; translating emerging societal needs into **connecting topics/themes or developing competencies across learning areas**; focusing on **conceptual understanding or "big ideas"** to avoid an excessive number of subjects and/or topics per subject – often described as "mile-wide, inch-deep"; carefully defining the pitch of what is included in curriculum; building in **coherent learning progressions** across grades; and **managing perceptions** by adjusting the size and/or format of curriculum documents.

"Connecting topics/themes or developing competencies across learning areas" is one of the main curriculum trends across schools and countries. On **cross-curricular themes**, the most frequently articulated across countries include "environmental education, sustainability" (57% of countries), "local and global citizenship, peace" (51% of countries), and "health education, well-being and lifestyle (51% of countries)". Among the least targeted cross-curricular themes are "regional and global engagement" (16%) and "media education" (11%). However, it would be misleading to only look at the thematic level. On c**ross-curricular competencies**, countries make different choices when embedding in existing subject areas:

- **ICT/digital literacy** has a stronger presence (on average, 40% of content items), in line with the growing movement towards digital transformation in education. It is emphasised in areas such as **technologies/home economics, national language, mathematics and science**. Estonia stands out because of the stronger emphasis (almost 70%), followed by Korea and Kazakhstan (just below 60%).

- Despite the growing needs for an interconnected world, **global competency** is explicitly articulated on average in 28% of content items, in areas such as **humanities, arts and national language**. This said, interdisciplinarity is acknowledged in several countries/jurisdictions by embedding it in areas such as **science** and **technologies/home economics**, and, although more rarely, in **mathematics** (in British Columbia [Canada], Korea, Northern Ireland [United Kingdom] and Sweden).

- With the increasing appearance of fake news, **media literacy** is highlighted as necessary competency for future. It is covered in around 24% of content items and is mostly emphasised in the areas of **national language** and **humanities**. Notable exceptions are two countries, Korea and Estonia for the degree of coverage (more than 50%), and two Canadian jurisdictions (British Columbia and Saskatchewan) for subject areas by emphasising it in **mathematics**.

- **Entrepreneurship** is only modestly embedded in curricula (on average 14% of curriculum). Estonia and Japan report a higher emphasis on entrepreneurship, with 40% and 56%, respectively, of the mapped curriculum targeting this competency. Both countries adopt a holistic approach by embedding entrepreneurship across most learning areas.

- With accelerated technological advancements such as *AI, Robotics, and Internet of Things*, **computational thinking/ programming/coding** is also embedded explicitly in curriculum but with a low percentage of content items (on average 11%) mainly in areas such as **technologies/home economics and mathematics**. The proportion is much higher in Estonia (37%) and the Russian Federation (32%).

- **Financial literacy** is one of the least targeted competencies (9%), mostly embedded in areas such as **technologies/home economics, humanities** and **mathematics**. Estonia and Kazakhstan give a greater emphasis to financial literacy (21% and 24%, respectively) and in a wider variety of learning areas.

Five key lessons learned from unintended consequences that countries experienced when tackling overload suggest to:

1. **keep the right balance between breadth of learning areas and depth of content knowledge**. Changing content often presents trade-offs; selecting only certain academic subjects to avoid overload can overlook the importance of "whole student development", "whole-school learning", and "whole community learning"; at the same time, keeping everything in limited space can lead to a "mile-wide, inch-deep" curriculum, creating a sense of disengagement in both students and teachers;

2. **use focus, rigour and coherence jointly as key design principles when addressing curriculum overload**, as using them as a package can help manage a false perception that focusing on a small number of topics leads to lowering standards, and ensure each student progresses their learning at developmentally appropriate levels;

3. **be conscious and avoid homework overload for students.** When contents are not covered during class, teachers are likely to assign homework, which disproportionately affects disadvantaged students, especially as types of homework are becoming more diverse. It also adversely influences teachers by increasing teachers' workload for homework preparation and marking.

What does research say?

WHAT IS CURRICULUM OVERLOAD?

Time is a finite resource for both students and teachers, and students and teachers often feel that a curriculum is crowded or overloaded. When addressing the issue of curriculum overload, curriculum designers frequently face questions such as: "Is it real or perceived?"; "How can we accommodate new demands from society in an already crowded curriculum?"; and "How can we ensure breadth and depth of learning that are both achievable within the time allocated in a curriculum?".

Drawing on the existing literature to address these questions, curriculum overload can be analysed within four dimensions (Box 1).

Box 1 **Four dimensions of curriculum overload**

1. **Curriculum expansion** refers to the tendency to include new content items in the curriculum in response to new societal demands without appropriately considering what items need to be removed.

2. **Content overload** refers to the actual dimension of curriculum overload, rather than as it perceived or experienced (i.e. the excessive amount of content to be taught and learned in relation to the time available for instruction).

3. **Perceived overload** refers to the perceived or experienced dimension of overload, as reported by teachers and students.

4. **Curriculum imbalance** refers to disproportionate attention given to certain areas of the curriculum at the expense of others without appropriate adjustments in the low-priority areas.

Curriculum overload is also known as curriculum overcrowding or curriculum expansion (Voogt, Nieveen and Klopping, 2017[1]). It has been reported by researchers in both developed and developing countries, including Angola, Australia[1], People's Republic of China, England (United Kingdom), Indonesia, Japan, Kenya, Malawi, the Netherlands, New Zealand, the Philippines, Tanzania, Viet Nam, Wales (United Kingdom), Zambia and Zimbabwe (Majoni, 2017[2]).

It is important to note that **curriculum overload is not the same as excessive workload for teachers and school leaders**. Many factors other than the curriculum have an impact on teacher workload, such as changes in administrative structure or student population (Easthope and Easthope, 2000[3]).

This section introduces definitions of these concepts and presents policy considerations as well as research findings on possible impacts of these dimensions on students and teachers. It concludes with a list of areas where additional research can inform how to close knowledge gaps and better inform policies addressing the issue of curriculum overload.

WHAT IS CURRICULUM EXPANSION? HOW DOES IT AFFECT STUDENTS AND TEACHERS?

Curriculum expansion refers to the tendency to include new content items in the curriculum as a response to new societal demands without proper consideration of what needs to be removed. Content expansion is cumulative and often occurs without attempts to remove prior content. Thus curricula become overcrowded over time (Alexander and Flutter, 2009[4]; Kärner et al., 2014[5]; Kuiper, Nieveen and Berkvens, 2013[6]; Voogt, Nieveen and Klopping, 2017[1]; Morgan and Craith, 2015[7]). This can occur due to new societal demands or pressure from lobby groups and a general desire to retain what has always been included in the curriculum. Such societal demands create new pressures on curriculum and teachers.

New societal demands

In our fast-changing world, there are increasing demands on the curriculum to reflect changes in society. Including emerging societal demands, such as digital literacy, financial literacy, literacy for sustainable development and computational thinking, can add a refreshing sense of relevance to what students are expected to learn (Kuiper, Nieveen and Berkvens, 2013[6]). For example, in Japan, the 2017 reform expanded the curriculum to cover content related to languages and computer programming and further increased instruction time, in response to growing demands for globalisation and algorithm/AI/computational thinking. In 2018, as part of its reference framework for quality learning, the European Commission highlighted a set of eight competencies deemed critical for lifelong learning:

- literacy
- multilingualism
- numerical, scientific and engineering skills
- digital and technology-based competences
- interpersonal skills and the ability to adopt new competences
- active citizenship
- entrepreneurship
- cultural awareness and expression (European Commission, 2018[8])

To compete for curriculum space, various actors and interest groups add pressure to reflect their agenda in the curriculum. Oates (2011[9]) also lists competing policy interests on what should be included in the core curriculum as one of the main reasons for overcrowding the national curriculum in England (United Kingdom). Curriculum may also become overcrowded when governments attempt to represent and accommodate all interest groups (Australian Primary Principals Association, 2014[10])[2]. Rawling (2015[11]) for example, points out how England's geography curriculum has been increasingly used for political control, with politically sensitive topics such as climate change added or removed with little consultation with subject knowledge specialists, based on lobbying by various interest groups.

Such demands and pressures may contribute to curriculum expansion, as content priority is sacrificed to meet the political necessity of breadth in coverage (Australian Primary Principals Association, 2014[10]; Kirst, Anhalt and Marine, 1997[12])[3]. In England (United Kingdom), for example, the *Cambridge Primary Review Report* finds that, over time the "list of subjects has simply become longer and longer, and nothing has been removed to accommodate the newcomers" (Alexander and Flutter, 2009[4]). In the period between 1995 and 2010, the national curriculum had repeatedly expanded in response to new societal developments and challenges triggered by technologies, nutrition, media, environment and other fields of human activity (Oates, 2011[9]). Such curriculum expansion includes adding content updates, new subjects, new topics within subjects or new cross-curricular themes to the existing curriculum, and it contributes to curriculum overload, often setting overly ambitious learning goals.

Limited space in curriculum for accommodating new demands

Adding a new subject(s) is one of the high-stakes policy choice. Traditional subjects, such as reading, writing and literature, and mathematics, continue to appear as the main building blocks of curriculum in most countries. On average across OECD countries, around 53% of the curriculum in lower secondary education is devoted to four subjects: reading, writing and literature (15%); mathematics (12%); natural sciences (12%); and second and other languages (14%). The remaining time is distributed among "other" compulsory curriculum (38%) and compulsory flexible curriculum (9%) (Figure 1)[4]. This is true in most OECD countries, except in those where the curriculum does not prescribe learning time (e.g. the Netherlands and the United Kingdom), which gives schools and teachers considerable flexibility in terms of curriculum architecture (OECD, 2020[13]).

When assessing the risk of curriculum overload from adding a new subject, policy makers usually assess how this strategy will impact the experienced curriculum and how it will affect students' total learning time. They need to weigh the benefits of adding subjects against the current demands of the curriculum.

Unchanged teaching time over the last decade

Adding new topics within existing subjects is a policy alternative to adding new subjects. Embedding topics into what already exists is an option that is less politically charged, but this poses challenges for teachers. As a response to increasing societal demands, an increased number of themes and competencies are introduced in existing subjects (see "What kinds of cross-curricular themes do countries/jursidictions articulate to accommodate new demands?"), without removing much content.

Figure 1 **Instruction time per subject in general lower secondary education (2019)**

As a percentage of total compulsory instruction time, in public institutions

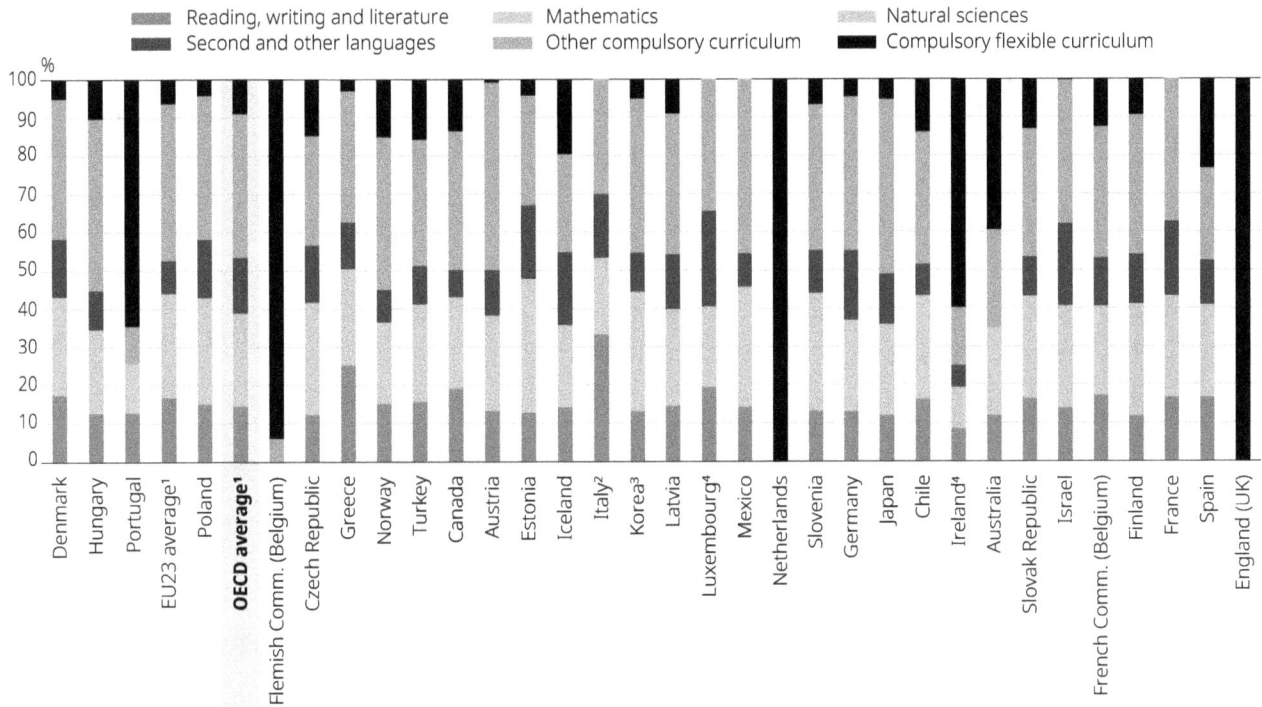

Notes: No marker for a country indicates that there are no data on the total number of compulsory instruction hours for one of the two corresponding reference years.

On 15 May 2020, the OECD Council invited Costa Rica to become a Member. While Costa Rica is included in the OECD averages reported in these tables and charts, at the time of its preparation, Costa Rica was in the process of completing its domestic procedures for ratification and the deposit of the instrument of accession to the OECD Convention was pending.

1. Excludes Australia (in 2014 only), England (United Kingdom), the Flemish Community of Belgium, Ireland (in 2019 only), the Netherlands and Portugal (in 2019 only).

2. Reading, writing and literature includes social studies. Mathematics includes natural sciences.

3. Natural sciences includes information and communication technologies and practical and vocational skills.

4. The second language of instruction includes other national languages taught in 2019.

Countries and economies are ranked in descending order of the percentage-point change in total compulsory instruction hours since 2014.

Source: (OECD, 2020[13]), Tables D1.2 and D1.4. See Source section for more information and Annex 3 for notes (https://doi.org/10.1787/69096873-en).

StatLink https://doi.org/10.1787/888934165282

Figure 2 shows the number of teaching hours per year in lower secondary education across countries and economies and over time. Although it shows considerable variation across countries, a point worth noting is that there is relatively little change in terms of the number of hours of instruction within each country from 2000 until 2018.

Teachers are thus required to integrate new themes or more content within the same amount of teaching time. As a result, students may face the risk of shallow learning if they are not allowed sufficient time to explore new concepts in a meaningful way.

New demands on teachers

Curriculum defines not only what students learn in school, but also how school can help them learn for life (OECD, 2019[14]; Abiko, 2019[15]). If students can see a sense of purpose in learning in their classroom (i.e. see the relevance of learning to what is needed in real life), they are likely to feel more motivated to learn and acquire the types of competencies teachers are trying to help them develop (Eccles and Midgley, 1989[16]). Their interest and engagement levels may be naturally higher than when learning traditional academic subjects. Greater levels of motivation can certainly facilitate student learning (Department of Education and Skills, 2015[17]). Students may feel a sense of relevance when the curriculum is more in line with real-world demands.

But teachers who have not received proper training may not know how to support students in these emerging areas. For example, at a time when digital skills are no longer considered merely "nice to have", but are rather deemed to be a core "must-have" competency for the future (OECD Learning Compass 2030 (OECD, 2019[18])), computational thinking and programming gain prominence in curriculum reform. However, teaching such skills requires specialised training. When teachers don't have that training, they are likely to feel overwhelmed and helpless (Rutherford, Long and Farkas, 2017[19]). Even well-prepared teachers may experience a drop in their sense of self-efficacy in some of these emerging areas if they have not received sufficient support through either their initial teacher preparation programme or targeted professional development activities (Zee and Koomen, 2016[20]).

Figure 2 **Number of teaching hours per year in general lower secondary education (2000, 2005 and 2018)**

Net statutory contact time in public institutions

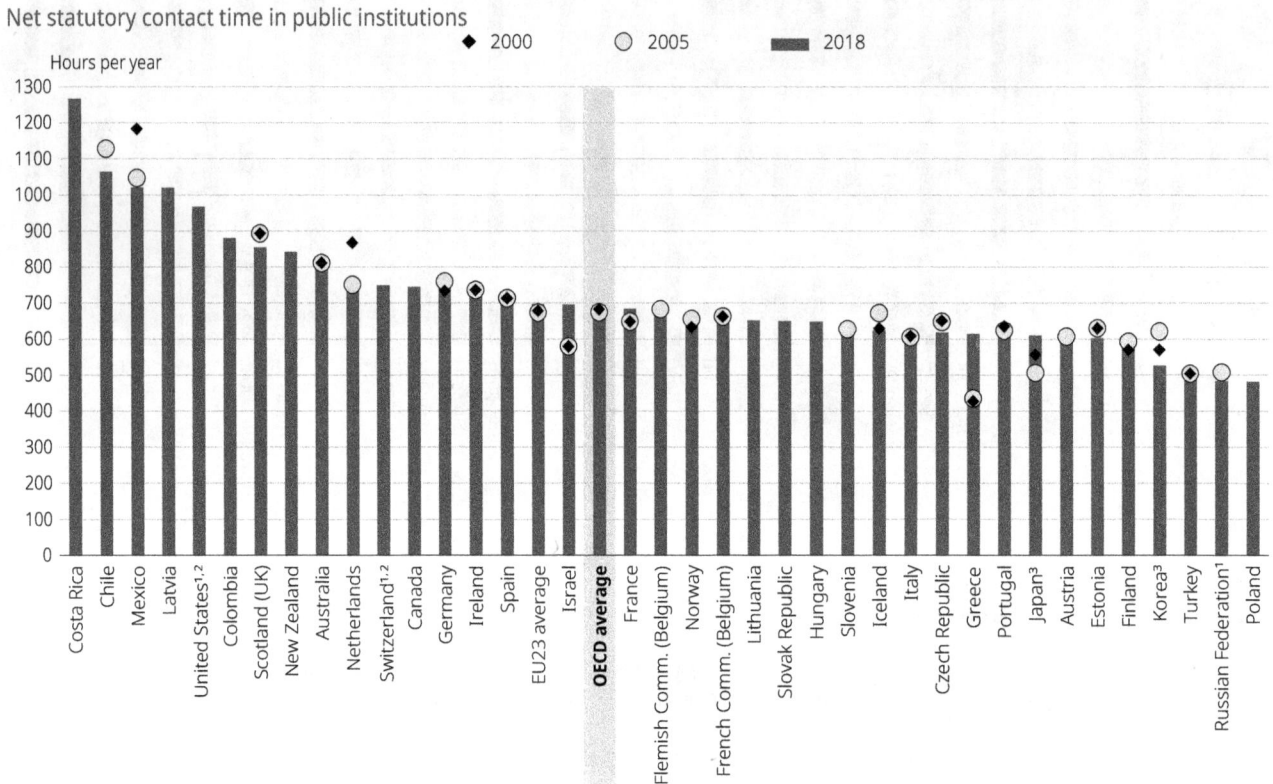

Note: In net statutory contact time in public institutions. The OECD and EU23 averages refer to countries and economies with available data for 2000, 2005, 2010, 2015 and 2018. Countries and economies are ranked in descending order of the number of teaching hours per year in general lower secondary education in 2018.

1. Actual teaching time.

2. Reference year differs from 2018. Refer to the source table for details.

3. Average planned teaching time in each school at the beginning of the school year or semester.

Source: Education at a Glance 2019: OECD Indicators, Figure D4.1, https://doi.org/10.1787/95fa0c1e-en.

StatLink ▨ https://doi.org/10.1787/888933980146

For example, data from the OECD Teaching and Learning International Survey (TALIS) reveal that supporting student learning through the use of digital technology is still a challenge for a large proportion of teachers who participated in the survey, compared with other typical skills (Figure 3).

Japan has also learned from past experience that expansion of content has additional complexities. The modernisation of subject content at the time was highly influenced by the work of J. S. Bruner's *The Process of Education* (Bruner, 1960[21]). The amount of learning contents reached a peak in the National Curriculum Standards revised from 1968 to 1970, which was pointed out that the Standards overemphasized on intellectual education. Subject content was partly redesigned to introduce the newest findings of natural and social sciences into school curriculum. Anecdotally, it has been reported that students struggled with the new content. The reasons for such unintended consequences are still unclear, but they seem to be linked to the levels of difficulty of the new content and the lack of teacher preparation for such new demands (Abiko, 2008[22]).

WHAT IS CONTENT OVERLOAD? HOW DOES IT AFFECT STUDENTS AND TEACHERS?

As noted earlier, resistance to accommodate new demands in curriculum partly comes from the difficulty in removing existing contents and subjects (Alexander and Flutter, 2009, p.17[4]). Content overload refers to the excessive amount of content to be taught and learned in relation to the time available for instruction (Boersma, 2001[23]). To avoid content overload, key considerations during curriculum redesign include: the overall structure of the curriculum; the number of subjects/topics; the quantity and quality of learning time; the pitch of what to include; and the size and language of curriculum documents.

Figure 3 **Percentage of lower secondary teachers who feel they can do the following "quite a bit" or "a lot" (OECD average-31)**

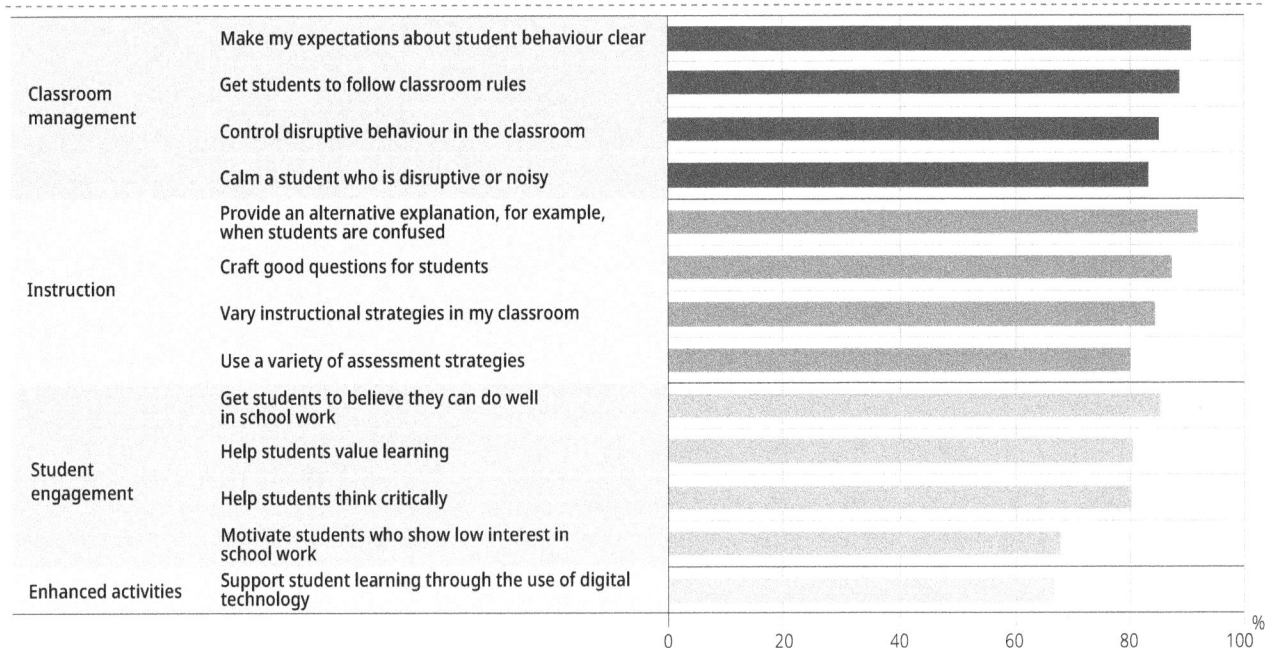

Source: OECD, TALIS 2018 Database, Table I.2.20

StatLink https://dx.doi.org/10.1787/888933932019

Structure and coherence

A poorly designed curriculum that lacks clear structure and coherence can increase the sense of content overload. When it is difficult to navigate through the curriculum, teachers are more likely to misunderstand its intent and use it ineffectively.

New Zealand has been considering how curriculum can be better designed to assist understanding and implementation. Drawing on the work of Graeme Aitken (Aitken, 2005[24]), the Ministry of Education put forward the following six criteria for evaluating the design of a curriculum statement (Ministry of Education (New Zealand), n.d.[25]):

1. It is logically structured around a clear and unambiguous purpose.

2. It clearly explains the rationale for change.

3. It incorporates misconception alerts.

4. It acknowledges teachers' existing understandings and integrates them into the new document.

5. It maximises internal coherence and minimises complexity.

6. It clearly connects abstract ideas to spatially contiguous detail and examples.

As noted above, what happens in a school is wider and more diverse in form than the stated content of a national curriculum. Content overload arises during curriculum redesign and becomes manifest during curriculum implementation (Boersma, 2001[23]), and it can be experienced differently by students, teachers and staff in the school (see "What is perceived overload? How does it affect students and teachers?").

Excessive number of subjects and/or topics per subject within the allotted time

The main challenge is when a curriculum contains an excessive number of subjects and/or topics within individual subjects (Voogt, Nieveen and Klopping, 2017[1]; Kärner et al., 2014[5]; Australian Primary Principals Association, 2014[10]; Haug, 2003[26]; NCCA, 2010[27]; FitzPatrick and O'Shea, 2013[28])[5]. Excessive content is commonly measured based on the analysis of instruction time allocated per content item (Schmidt, Wang and McKnight, 2005[29]; Schmidt, Houang and Cogan, 2002[30]). Research in cognitive science suggests that cognitive overload, associated with increased mental stress and reduced relaxation, results in decreased student performance (Fraser et al., 2012[31]).

Less is more: defining the right number of topics

Content overload is often driven by **unrealistic expectations for retaining both breadth and depth of content within the allotted space and time**. Breadth means the number of subjects included in the curriculum and the number of topics to be taught within subjects. Depth means the degree to which students explore and understand what they are learning.

Achieving an appropriate balance between breadth and depth in curriculum content remains a persistent unresolved issue in education reforms of many countries (Alexander, 2009[32]), with direct consequences for students' learning. Coverage of broad knowledge content is often prioritised over in-depth learning, which results in "more learning" rather than "deeper learning" (Schmidt and Houang, 2012[33]).

Having fewer topics to be covered in more depth in a curriculum often raises concerns about lowering standards of student achievement (UNESCO, 2002[34]). However, research suggests that studying fewer topics in greater depth helps students to develop richer understanding and higher-order thinking that can be transferred beyond specific subjects to new learning areas and new problems (Coker et al., 2016[35]; Schwartz et al., 2009[36]). Schwartz et al. (2009[36]), among others, argue that a focus on learning in depth may improve not only student academic achievement but also student satisfaction (Laird et al., 2008[37]).

Countries/jurisdictions include a wide variety of subjects in their curriculum. At the subject level, the secondary school curriculum of post-Soviet Ukraine in the 2000s included 17 different subjects, with as little as one hour of instruction per subject per week, while an average secondary school student in Uzbekistan studied as many as 28 different subjects (Moreno, 2007[38]). At the level of content items, a high number of topics within subjects has been cited as a major source of curriculum content overload in the United States. While eighth-grade mathematics textbooks in high-performing countries, such as Japan and Singapore, cover about 10 topics, those used in the United States cover as many as 30 topics (Schmidt, Houang and Cogan, 2002[30]). The mathematics and science curriculum in the United States has been criticised as "a mile wide and an inch deep". This approach to curriculum has been found to lead to poorer outcomes than in other countries in terms of student achievement (Schmidt, Houang and Cogan, 2002[30]; Schmidt and Houang, 2012[33]; Schmidt, Wang and McKnight, 2005[29]).

Prioritising some topics as key concepts in a crowded curriculum

An increasing number of countries/jurisdictions have made a clear distinction in curriculum between "key concepts" and "facts and procedural knowledge" to facilitate deeper learning. Accordingly, the concept of "big ideas" (similar to "key concepts", "fundamental ideas" or "essential learning") commonly appears in curricula as a way to highlight essential ideas that, approached from different angles, are crucial to multiple learning areas in both OECD countries and partner economies (Table 1). The simplicity of indicating clearly what are the "big ideas" in a learning area can help teachers remain focused when deciding what to prioritise from the more exhaustive curriculum without being overly prescriptive at the level of content items.

British Columbia (Canada) adopted this "big ideas" model in their curriculum redesign (Figure 4). The curriculum was designed by curriculum development teams that included teachers early in the process. The teams worked together through the revisions, which resulted in a progression of big ideas, curricular competencies and content for each learning area.

Unique to their approach is a clear indication of which content is to be prioritised. In this approach, greater value is placed on competencies and content that transfer across contexts and on a conscious effort to identify what is considered essential learning, among many items that could potentially be present in an exhaustive curriculum. This means, for example, prioritising higher-order concepts and ideas that are fundamental and enduring within a disciplinary body of knowledge and those that possess greater transfer value across disciplines and contexts.

This transferability supports the learning process across subjects in such a way that what students learn in science, for example, might support what they will be learning in social studies. This can be illustrated by the concept of "change", which in the British Columbia curriculum is considered to be transferrable across the subjects of arts education, social studies, science, health education/physical education and mathematics (Table 2).

Table 1 **Use of "big ideas" and key concepts**

Yes		No	
OECD	**Partner**	**OECD**	**Partner**
Australia	Brazil[1]	Lithuania	Argentina
British Columbia (Canada)	Hong Kong (China)	Netherlands	
Chile	Costa Rica		
Czech Republic	India[1]		
Denmark	Kazakhstan		
Estonia	Russian Federation		
Finland	Singapore		
Hungary	South Africa		
Ireland	Viet Nam		
Japan			
Korea			
New Zealand			
Northern Ireland (United Kingdom)[1]			
Norway			
Poland			
Portugal			
Ontario (Canada)			
Québec (Canada)			
Scotland (United Kingdom)			
Sweden			
Turkey			
Wales (United Kingdom)			

Note: Values displayed in this table include only countries/jurisdiction with responses that could be clearly coded as yes/no.

1. Responses for these countries/jurisdictions were submitted by independent researchers, not government administrations.

Source: Data from the PQC, item 1.1.3.2.

Figure 4 **"Big Ideas" from the lenses of competencies in the OECD Learning Compass 2030**

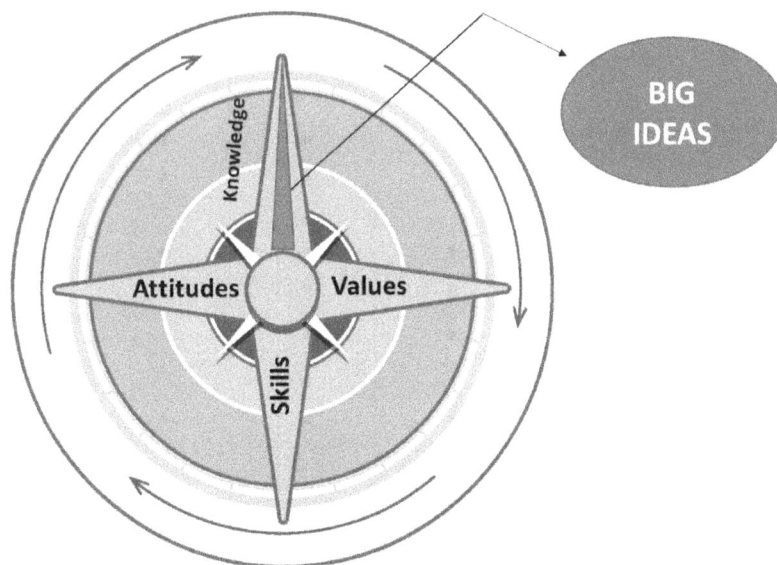

Source: Adapted from the "Big Ideas" in the British Columbia curriculum model (https://curriculum.gov.bc.ca/sites/curriculum.gov.bc.ca/files/pictures/curriculum_model.png), Education 2030 Conceptual Learning Framework: Background papers, p. 118, https://www.oecd.org/education/2030-project/contact/Conceptual_learning_framework_Conceptual_papers.pdf.

Table 2[1/2] **"Big ideas" across learning areas in the curriculum, British Columbia (Canada)**

	ELA	Arts Education	Social Studies	Science	HE/PE	Mathematics	FRALP
Adapt/Adaptation			•	•			
Authority			•				
Balance		•					
Cause and Effect/Consequence			•	•	•		
Change		•	•	•	•	•	
Choice			•		•		
Classify/Classification				•	•	•	
Cooperation			•		•		
Community		•	•	•			•
Conflict/Crisis		•	•		•		
Contact			•				
Culture	•	•	•	•			•
Cycles			•	•			
Ecosystems				•			
Energy		•	•	•	•		
Environment			•	•			•
Ethics		•	•	•			
Evolution			•	•			
Forces				•	•		
Form	•	•	•	•	•		•
Form and Function				•			
Genre	•						•
Harmony		•					
Identity	•	•	•		•		•
Innovation			•	•			
Interactions		•	•	•	•		
Interdependence			•				
Matter and Energy				•			
Meaning	•						
Motion		•		•	•		
Needs			•	•			
Order			•	•			
Organize			•				
Pattern		•	•	•	•	•	
Place	•	•	•				
Point of View/Perspective	•	•	•				
Power			•				
Processes		•	•	•			
Probability						•	
Properties				•			

Note: ELA – English language arts; HE/PE – Health education/Physical education; FRALP – Français langue première.

Source: Education 2030 – Conceptual Learning Framework: Background papers, p. 137, https://www.oecd.org/education/2030-project/contact/Conceptual_learning_framework_Conceptual_papers.pdf.

Table 2[2/2] **"Big ideas" across learning areas in the curriculum, British Columbia (Canada)**

	ELA	Arts Education	Social Studies	Science	HE/PE	Mathematics	FRALP
Relationship		•	•		•	•	
Resiliency			•				
Resources			•				
Responsibility		•	•		•		
Role	•	•	•		•		•
Society		•	•				
Space		•		•		•	
Stories	•	•	•				
Systems and Structures	•	•	•	•			•
Sustainability			•	•			
Time	•	•	•			•	
Traditions		•	•	•			
Transform		•		•		•	
Unity		•					
Voice	•	•					
Worldviews		•	•				

Note: ELA – English language arts; HE/PE – Health education/Physical education; FRALP – Français langue première.

Source: Education 2030 – Conceptual Learning Framework: Background papers, p. 137, https://www.oecd.org/education/2030-project/contact/Conceptual_learning_framework_Conceptual_papers.pdf.

The New Zealand curriculum provides only high-level guidance. Subject-specific content is not mandated, although key topics and focus areas are identified. For example, the following key topics are included in the Science learning area: New Zealand flora and fauna; interdependence of geosphere, hydrosphere, atmosphere and biosphere; and physical phenomena such as light, sound, heat, motion, waves and forces. In a few instances, the government advises on the importance of including specific content. But, in general, most decisions regarding the selection of topics within each learning area are left to schools guided by the structure of the learning area and the achievement objectives set out in the national curriculum.

In New Zealand, the national curriculum is composed of the New Zealand Curriculum and *Te Marautanga o Aotearoa* (TMOA). Both documents are the result of broad societal consultation, including the views of teachers, principals, school boards, parents, employer representatives, curriculum associations, education sector bodies, academics and the wider community. TMOA is a guide to teaching practices in Māori-medium schools in New Zealand. It is merely a framework, not a complete teaching plan or teaching programme. Here again, schools need to develop their own school-based curriculum. For example, programmes may be planned by learning area, topic or context. Both the New Zealand Curriculum and TMOA succinctly describe what is considered essential for learning. Schools are expected to develop and design their own curriculum based on broad specifications.

In the United States, at the suggestion of the National Science Foundation, a number of award-winning scientists convened to discuss what could be considered "fundamental ideas" in science and how they could be the basis for a new science curriculum. The result was The "8+1" Fundamental Ideas of Science (Figure 5). These fundamental ideas represent answers to three questions:

- How do we know what we know?
- What are things made of?
- How do systems interact and change?

The "+1" (meaning "Inquiry") is related to essential ideas, such as probability, scientific reasoning, scales, measurement and orders of magnitude. The new curriculum could in turn embrace the principles of focus, rigour and coherence (Schmidt, 2011[39]). As design principles to guide curriculum contstruction, *focus* suggests that a relatively small number of topics should be introduced to ensure deep, quality learning; *rigour* suggests that topics should be challenging and enable deep thinking and reflection, which is not to be confused with rigid or inflexible design; and *coherence* suggests that topics should be ordered in a logical way to create a progression (OECD, 2019[40])

Figure 5 **The 8+1 Fundamental Ideas of Science**

The 8+1 Fundamental Ideas of Science
Preamble : What is science ? What is science for ?

- Science is able to explain how the natural world works by means of a small number of laws of nature.
- These laws, often expressed mathematically, are explored using tools such as observation, measurement, and description.
- Information is synthesized into understanding through creative thought and with predictions continuously tested by observation and measurement.

How do we know what we know?
Inquiry (+1)

Of what are things made?	How do systems interact and change?
1. Everything is made of atoms and atoms are composed of subatomic particles.	4. Evolution: Systems evolve and change with time according to simple underlying rules or laws.
2. Cells are the basic units of organisms.	5. Parts of a system move and interact with each other through forces.
3. Electromagnetic radiation pervades our world.	6. Parts of a system can exchange energy and matter when they interact.
	7. Physical concepts like energy and mass can be stored and transformed but are never created or destroyed.
	8. Life systems evolve through variation.

Source: (Schmidt, 2011[39])

In mathematics, some countries/jurisdictions are also shifting away from disconnected factual knowledge towards more holistic conceptual understanding to make mathematical learning more meaningful to students. Word problems have long been used to convey real-world situations, which help students understand how mathematical concepts can be used outside of school (OECD, 2014[41]). Examples include problems on purchasing furniture with a discount and determining someone's age based on a relationship to the age of others.

Emerging 21st century challenges are also reinforcing the need to foster a deeper conceptual understanding of mathematical content as opposed to rote learning. Addressing these challenges requires equipping students to think mathematically (OECD, 2014[41]). Many countries are fostering conceptual understanding by giving students opportunities to learn different kinds of formal mathematical concepts, such as calculus, complex numbers and trigonometry.

Increased mathematical reasoning and the ability to apply problems in the real world have to go hand in hand. Nonetheless, in already crowded curricula, it is often difficult to make sufficient room for opportunities to learn for both and countries/jurisdictions need to set priorities. Deeper understanding of mathematical concepts is linked to being able to apply mathematical reasoning and problem solving. While word problems are often easier for teachers to apply, they may be more prone to rote learning than to deep learning.

Figure 6 shows how countries/jurisdictions seem to be making different choices in their mathematics curriculum based on students' reported exposure to either word problems or formal mathematics, which supports conceptual understanding. For example, students in Shanghai (China), a high-performing PISA jurisdiction, report the greatest exposure to conceptual understanding through formal mathematics while being much less exposed to word problems among participating countries and economies. In contrast, Iceland shows the opposite pattern: their students are frequently exposed to word problems with comparatively few chances of being exposed to formal mathematics. When faced with limited time, the choices of what to prioritise can make a difference for the type of learning students will experience and how enduring their learning is within and across disciplinary boundaries.

Figure 6 **Exposure to word problems and conceptual understanding**

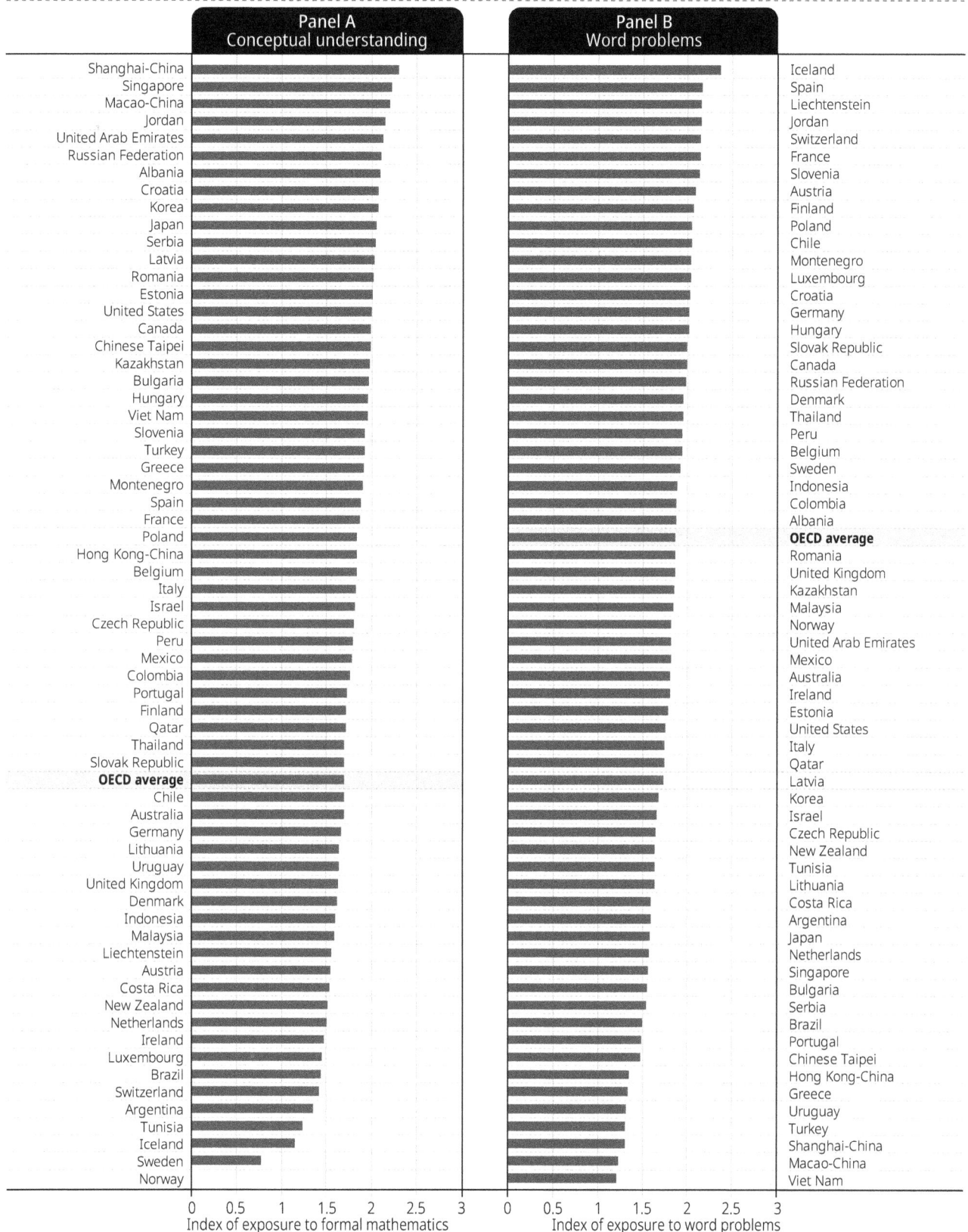

Panel A Conceptual understanding	Panel B Word problems
Shanghai-China	Iceland
Singapore	Spain
Macao-China	Liechtenstein
Jordan	Jordan
United Arab Emirates	Switzerland
Russian Federation	France
Albania	Slovenia
Croatia	Austria
Korea	Finland
Japan	Poland
Serbia	Chile
Latvia	Montenegro
Romania	Luxembourg
Estonia	Croatia
United States	Germany
Canada	Hungary
Chinese Taipei	Slovak Republic
Kazakhstan	Canada
Bulgaria	Russian Federation
Hungary	Denmark
Viet Nam	Thailand
Slovenia	Peru
Turkey	Belgium
Greece	Sweden
Montenegro	Indonesia
Spain	Colombia
France	Albania
Poland	**OECD average**
Hong Kong-China	Romania
Belgium	United Kingdom
Italy	Kazakhstan
Israel	Malaysia
Czech Republic	Norway
Peru	United Arab Emirates
Mexico	Mexico
Colombia	Australia
Portugal	Ireland
Finland	Estonia
Qatar	United States
Thailand	Italy
Slovak Republic	Qatar
OECD average	Latvia
Chile	Korea
Australia	Israel
Germany	Czech Republic
Lithuania	New Zealand
Uruguay	Tunisia
United Kingdom	Lithuania
Denmark	Costa Rica
Indonesia	Argentina
Malaysia	Japan
Liechtenstein	Netherlands
Austria	Singapore
Costa Rica	Bulgaria
New Zealand	Serbia
Netherlands	Brazil
Ireland	Portugal
Luxembourg	Chinese Taipei
Brazil	Hong Kong-China
Switzerland	Greece
Argentina	Uruguay
Tunisia	Turkey
Iceland	Shanghai-China
Sweden	Macao-China
Norway	Viet Nam

Index of exposure to formal mathematics / Index of exposure to word problems

Note: Panel A shows students exposure to conceptual understanding according to the results of PISA 2012. The exposure to conceptual understanding of mathematics is operationalised as an index of exposure to formal mathematics ranging from 0 (never) to 3 (frequently). Panel B shows students exposure to word problems according to the results of PISA 2012. The exposure to word problems is operationalised as an index of exposure to word problems ranging from 0 (never) to 3 (frequently). For more information on how these indices are constructed see (OECD, 2014[41]).

Source: PISA 2012 Database, Tables I.3.1a and I.3.1b, https://doi.org/10.1787/9789264267510-en.

StatLink https://doi.org/10.1787/888934195739

Reinforcing the notion of "big ideas", "fundamental ideas", and "conceptual understanding' is the concept of "essential learning" as seen earlier in the case of the British Columbia new curriculum. In their framework, the definition of what constitutes essential learning varies by learning area, but it should result from a reflection on what students should know (knowledge, facts) within a learning area, what essential ideas students should understand and use in other contexts, and what students should be able to do in a learning area or across learning areas as a result of learning at a given grade level. The principles[6] include the following (OECD, 2017[42]):

- Pay close attention to the important concepts and big ideas in each area of learning to support the application and transfer of essential learning.

- Ensure that core competencies are explicitly considered in the renewed curriculum to support deeper learning and the transfer of key skills and processes to new contexts.

- Limit the amount of prescription while ensuring a solid focus on essential learning.

- Stress higher-order learning, giving emphasis to the key concepts and enduring understandings (big ideas) that students need to succeed in their education and their lives.

- Allow for flexibility and choice for teachers and students.

Focusing on big ideas and essential learning is one of the common strategies used by countries to mitigate content overload. This will also help facilitate effective learning by keeping the developmental needs of children in mind.

Connecting topics across different subjects for real-world issues

Making connections across subjects (e.g. through cross-curricular themes and competencies) can be an effective strategy of reinforcing content and deep learning (Hurley, 2001[43]). Early childhood education curriculum is not organised by subjects in the first place and, thus, it does not need to break down silos between subjects (Jenkins et al., 2019[44]). However, secondary education teachers may not feel prepared to implement cross-curricular connections, even immediately after their training (Parker, Heywood and Jolley, 2012[45]). In primary education, it is easier to implement the approach as the same teacher teaches all subjects. However, given accountability measures, primary teachers may also find making these connections a challenge (Brand and Triplett, 2012[46]).

Project-based learning can be a model to integrate different subjects and make meaningful connections. These are cross-curricular projects wherein students solve a real-world problem or participate in a group project. They make connections across subjects like science, mathematics and writing, because they need to conduct the project, write up and present material, and solve the problem. Indeed, such approaches can improve learning and attitudes, through the group-oriented nature of the work (Kaldi, Filippatou and Govaris, 2011[47]). Various approaches and methods can be used to facilitate learning, but project-based learning often feels more relevant to students and can be effective at engaging them (Kokotsaki, Menzies and Wiggins, 2016[48]), while there is no conclusive evidence on the impact of such practices on actual learning outcomes.

Coherence among topics across grades, learning cycles and education levels

Research in neuroscience highlights the **value of staging new content** so that the brain can appropriately organise information for deeper understanding (Simon and Tzur, 2004[49]; Simon et al., 2010[50]; Lehrer and Schauble, 2015[51]; Penuel and Shepard, 2016[52]; Shepard, Penuel and Pellegrino, 2018[53]; Giedd, 2004[54]). When introducing new content in a curriculum, prominent attention should be given to **staging or sequencing the new topics**, taking into account students' stress (e.g. feeling overwhelmed by too many materials that are too difficult for them) or boredom (e.g. repeating materials they already understand).

Some repetition of topics is deliberate. It is built into a curriculum to reinforce students' understanding of the ideas or concepts they are learning. If the prerequisite notions have not been properly taught or understood, this may hinder their understanding of new content. This could occur by not paying sufficient attention to what students are presumed to know and what they have actually understood at the start of each grade or level.

Other repetition of topics is considered duplication of content. This is reported as a challenge by countries/jurisdictions such as Australia, Korea and the Netherlands. Some have started to limit such duplication by reducing content or taking an interdisciplinary approach. Most others report using learning progressions (Table 3). In particular, Estonia, Ireland and New Zealand adopted the approach to recognise the non-linear nature and individual differences in learning progressions, rather than organising learning linearly by grades. This is often called a "**spiral curriculum**" (See "What types of challenges do countries/jurisdictions face in addressing curriculum overload, and what strategies do they use to address these challenges?").

Several report challenges not only in content duplication but also in the disconnect in learning progression between different levels of education. One of the strategies to address the repetition of content and disconnect across grades, is to redefine leaning goals by learning stages rather than grades, such as by primary or secondary cycle, as well as by achievement levels or by other factors such as discipline or level of complexity. This allows opportunities to review and repeat content throughout the different grades in accordance with the level of the learner's development (see"What types of challenges do countries/jurisdictions face in addressing curriculum overload, and what strategies do they use to address these challenges?" section for country examples).

Curriculum progression may refer not only to the transition from simple to complex ideas. It may also be used to help students move from concrete examples to more abstract levels of thinking. These progressions represent a long-term plan of trajectories for students' learning over the years, rather than a grade-by-grade approach and, as such, they are more of an adaptive process (Confrey, 2019[55]).

When curriculum frameworks for each level of education are supported by a coherent, longer span of age coverage, alignment across different education levels becomes easier to achieve. Without such a framework, curriculum committees at each different level of education are likely to make decisions considering the age group specific to that level. This often results in fragmentation, redundancies and inconsistency of topics across levels of education.

Furthermore, it is important to be mindful of students' development across education levels. Curriculum that is primarily built on the priorities of subject areas rather than on what is developmentally appropriate is likely to overlook grade-level transitions and could allow repetition to persist without considering or assessing the needs of students (Eccles and Midgley, 1989[16]). Students may experience a decreased sense of self-efficacy, along with negative attributions to explain failure in the face of new learning (Schunk and Dibenedettto, 2016[56]; Zhen et al., 2010[57]).

Students may start to believe that they are not smart enough to learn the new material (Wigfield et al., 1997[58]). This can lead them to simply stop trying and to develop fixed ideas rather than an enquiring mind (Weiner, 1972[59]). Repeating topics can help students bridge old and new learning. Focus, rigour and coherence remain the critical design principles when considering the amount, level, and sequencing of topics to include in a curriculum (see Overview Brochure)[7].

In Denmark and Sweden, for example, the curriculum framework encompasses primary and lower secondary education in a coherent way, considering and accommodating learning progressions (Figure 7). This helps to avoid fragmentation and content overlaps which can put unnecessary pressure in curricula, increasing curriculum overload and potentially causing students to disengage.

Table 3 **Student learning progressions in the curriculum across different levels of education**

Yes		No	
OECD	Partner	OECD	Partner
Australia	Brazil[1]	Hungary	Viet Nam
British Columbia (Canada)	Hong Kong (China)	Netherlands	
Chile	Costa Rica		
Czech Republic	Kazakhstan		
Estonia	Singapore		
Finland	South Africa		
Japan			
Korea			
Lithuania			
Mexico			
New Zealand			
Northern Ireland (United Kingdom)[1]			
Norway			
Ontario (Canada)			
Poland			
Portugal			
Québec (Canada)			
Scotland (United Kingdom)			
Sweden			
Wales (United Kingdom)			

Note: Values displayed in this table include only countries/jurisdictions with responses that could be clearly coded as yes/no.

1. Responses for these countries/jurisdictions were submitted by independent researchers, not government administrations.

Source: Data from the PQC, item 1.6.

Figure 7 [1/6] Age coverage of curriculum frameworks across different levels of education

This table captures the coverage of different curriculum frameworks by age band and ISCED level.

Legend: ISCED level 0 | ISCED level 1 | ISCED level 2 | ISCED level 3 | Overlap of age group | frameworks across multiple ISCED levels | not mandatory

	0 year-olds (1)	1 year-olds (2)	2 year-olds (3)	3 year-olds (4)	4 year-olds (5)	5 year-olds (6)	6 year-olds (7)	7 year-olds (8)	8 year-olds (9)	9 year-olds (10)
Austria	0-6 year-olds (Kindergarten, Pre-school)							7-10 year-olds (Voekschule/Primary)		
Australia			2-5 year-olds (Early Years Learning Framework)				5-12 year-olds (The Australian Curriculum)			
British Columbia (Canada)[3]						British Columbia Kindergarten Curriculum	British Columbia Curriculum: Elementary Education			
Chile	Bases Curriculares de Educación Pavularia (Early Childhood Education Curricular Bases) (0-5 yrs 11 mths)							Bases Curriculares para la Educación Básica (Curricular Bases for Primary Education)		
Czech Republic			Framework Educational Programme for Preschool Education (FEP PE)					Framework Educational Programme for Basic Education (FEP BE)		
			Framework Educational Programme for Preschool Education (FEP PE)							
Denmark	0-5 year-olds (Pædagogiske læreplaner / pedagogical curriculum)						6-16 years (Fælles Mål (Common Objectives) for each grade in primary school, including preschool class)			
Estonia			18mth-6 year-olds (National Curriculum for Preschool Child Care Institutions)					7-12 year-olds (National Curriculum for Basic Schools)		
Finland	0-6 years (Varhaiskasvatusuunnitelman Perusteet / National curriculum guidelines on early childhood education and care)						Esiopetuksen Opetussuun-nitelman Perusteet (National Core Curriculum for Pre-primary education)	7-12 year-olds		
								Perusopetuksen Opetussuunnitelman Perusteet (National Core Curriculum for Basic Education) 7-15 year-olds		
Hungary	0-3 year-olds (A bölcsődei nevelés-gondozás szakmai szabályai / National Guidance for the education and care of children under the age of 3)			3-6/7 year-olds (Óvodai nevelés országos alapprogramja / National Basic Programme for Kindergarten Education)				6-10 year-olds (Nemzeti alaptanterv + Kerettantervek / National Core Curriculum + Framework Curricula - up-18)		
Israel				3-6 year-olds (Preschool + Kindergarten)				6-12 year-olds (Primary)		
Ireland				3-6 year-olds				6-12 year-olds		
	Early Childhood Curriculum Framework: Aistear (up to 6 year-olds)							Primary Curriculum		
Japan				3-6 year-olds (National Curriculum Standard)				7-12 year-olds (National Curriculum Standard)		
	National curriculum of daycare centre									

Notes: Curriculum frameworks for the different ISCED levels (0 to 3) are shown as bars in increasingly darker shades of blue. Overlaps between different ISCED-level frameworks are marked in dark grey. The figure further depicts overarching curriculum frameworks reported by countries/jurisdictions that do not necessarily correspond to just one ISCED level, which are shown as white boxes with a black frame. Education levels that are non-mandatory are highlighted in light grey. Age brackets where there is no framework coverage are left blank.

1. Data submitted by researcher not governmental institution.

2. United States: Individual states determine their own curricula structure. In many states, local school districts make all curriculum decisions.

3. ISCED levels shown are only provided as a general indication, and do not represent ISCED reporting for Canada as a whole. Additionally, this information only reflects the formal public K-12 system for each.

Source: Data from the PQC, item 0.3

StatLink ᴍꜱᴾ https://doi.org/10.1787/888934195758

Figure 7 [2/6] Age coverage of curriculum frameworks across different levels of education

This table captures the coverage of different curriculum frameworks by age band and ISCED level.

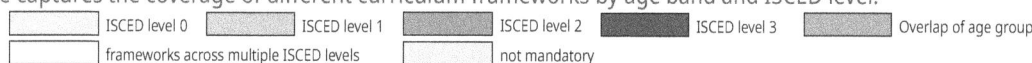

ISCED level 0	ISCED level 1	ISCED level 2	ISCED level 3	Overlap of age group
frameworks across multiple ISCED levels	not mandatory			

10 year-olds (11)	11 year-olds (12)	12 year-olds (13)	13 year-olds (14)	14 year-olds (15)	15 year-olds (16)	16 year-olds (17)	17 year-olds (18)	18 year-olds (19)	19 year-olds (20)		
7-10 year-olds (Voekschule/ Primary)	11-14 year-olds (Neue Mittelschule, Allgemeinbildende höhere Schule (AHS))				15-18 year-olds (AHS, Berufsbildende höhere Schule (BHS))				BHS	Austria	OECD
5-12 year-olds (The Australian Curriculum)		12-16 year-olds					16-18 year-olds			Australia	
The Australian Curriculum + courses developed by states and territories											
British Columbia Curriculum: Elementary Education			British Columbia Curriculum: Secondary Education, Grades 7-9			British Columbia Curriculum: Secondary Education, Grades 10-12				British Columbia (Canada)[3]	
Bases Curriculares para la Educación Básica (Curricular Bases for Primary Education)										Chile	
Framework Educational Programme for Basic Education (FEP BE)	Framework Educational Programme for Basic Education (FEP BE)									Czech Republic	
6-16 years (Fælles Mål (Common Objectives) for each grade in primary school, including preschool class)							General Upper Secondary (læreplaner curriculum) / Vocational Upper Secondary Education (lokale læreplaner, local curriculum)			Denmark	
7-12 year-olds (National Curriculum for Basic Schools)			13-15 year-olds (National Curriculum for Basic Schools)			16-19 year-olds (National Curriculum for Upper Secondary Schools)				Estonia	
7-12 year-olds			13-15 year-olds (National Curriculum for Basic Schools)			16-19 year-olds (National Core Curriculum for General Upper Secondary Education, ages 16-18/19 Lukion Opetussuunnitelman Perusteet OR National Qualification Requirements for Vocational Education and Training, ages 16-18/19 Ammatillisen Koulutuksen Tutkintojen Perusteet)				Finland	
Perusopetuksen Opetussuunnitelman Perusteet (National Core Curriculum for Basic Education) 7-15 year-olds											
10-14 year-olds					14-18 year-olds (subject-changes based on the current curriculum reform					Hungary	
6-12 year-olds (Primary)			13-15 year-olds (Middle School)			16-18 year-olds (High School)				Israel	
6-12 year-olds			12-16 year-olds				16-18 year-olds			Ireland	
Primary Curriculum			Junior Cycle Framework				Senior Cycle				
7-12 year-olds (National Curriculum Standard)			13-15 year-olds (National Curriculum Standard for Junior High School)			16-18 year-olds (National Curriculum Standard for High School)				Japan	

Notes: Curriculum frameworks for the different ISCED levels (0 to 3) are shown as bars in increasingly darker shades of blue. Overlaps between different ISCED-level frameworks are marked in dark grey. The figure further depicts overarching curriculum frameworks reported by countries/jurisdictions that do not necessarily correspond to just one ISCED level, which are shown as white boxes with a black frame. Education levels that are non-mandatory are highlighted in light grey. Age brackets where there is no framework coverage are left blank.

1. Data submitted by researcher not governmental institution.

2. United States: Individual states determine their own curricula structure. In many states, local school districts make all curriculum decisions.

3. ISCED levels shown are only provided as a general indication, and do not represent ISCED reporting for Canada as a whole. Additionally, this information only reflects the formal public K-12 system for each.

Source: Data from the PQC, item 0.3

StatLink 🖳 https://doi.org/10.1787/888934195758

Figure 7 [3/6] Age coverage of curriculum frameworks across different levels of education

This table captures the coverage of different curriculum frameworks by age band and ISCED level.

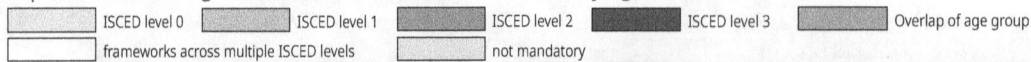

Legend: ISCED level 0 | ISCED level 1 | ISCED level 2 | ISCED level 3 | Overlap of age group | frameworks across multiple ISCED levels | not mandatory

	0 year-olds (1)	1 year-olds (2)	2 year-olds (3)	3 year-olds (4)	4 year-olds (5)	5 year-olds (6)	6 year-olds (7)	7 year-olds (8)	8 year-olds (9)	9 year-olds (10)
Latvia		1.5 - 6 year-olds (Preschool Education Guidelines)						7-15/16 year-olds (Basic Education Standard)		
Lithuania	0 - 6 year-olds (Pre-school)							7-10 year-olds (Primary)		
Luxembourg					4-6 year-olds (Cycle 1)			7-11 year-olds (Cycle 1 & 2 & 3)		
Korea		누리과정 (Nuri Curriculum) (not mandatory)					6-11 year-olds(National Elementary School Curriculum)			
Mexico	0-3 year-olds (Modelo de Atención con Enfoque Integral para la Educación Inicial / National Guidance for the education and care of children under the age of 3)			3-5 year-olds (Pre-school)			6-11 year-olds (Primary)			
Netherlands					4-12 year-olds (doelen* Objectives)					
New Zealand	Te Whāriki (early childhood curriculum)					Curriculum and Te Marautanga o Aotearoa (the national curriculum for Māori medium schooling) up-18				
Northern Ireland (United Kingdom)[1]					4-11 year-olds					
Norway		1-6 year-olds (Rammeplan for barnehagens innhold og oppgaver / Framework Plan for the Content and Tasks of Kindergartens)						6-12 year-olds (Kunnskapsløftet 2020 (KL20) / Knowledge Promotion 2020)		
Ontario (Canada)[3]					The Kindergarten Program		The Ontario Curriculum: Elementary			
Poland				3-7 year-olds				7-15 year-olds		
Portugal				3-5 year-olds (Pre-primary)			6-9 year-olds (Primary)			
Québec (Canada)[3]					QEP: Preschool Education Program for 4-Year-Olds and Preschool Education Program		Québec Education Program (QEP): Elementary			
Sweden	0-5 year-olds (Läroplan för förskolan / Lpfö 18, revised 2018 / Curriculum for the Preschool)						6-9 year-olds / 6-15 year-olds (Curriculum for the compulsory school, preschool class and school-age educare - revised 2018)			
Turkey	prior to school						Primary School (grades 1-4)			
Wales (United Kingdom)	(m)									
United States[1,2]										

(OECD — left margin label)

Notes: Curriculum frameworks for the different ISCED levels (0 to 3) are shown as bars in increasingly darker shades of blue. Overlaps between different ISCED-level frameworks are marked in dark grey. The figure further depicts overarching curriculum frameworks reported by countries/jurisdictions that do not necessarily correspond to just one ISCED level, which are shown as white boxes with a black frame. Education levels that are non-mandatory are highlighted in light grey. Age brackets where there is no framework coverage are left blank.

1. Data submitted by researcher not governmental institution.

2. United States: Individual states determine their own curricula structure. In many states, local school districts make all curriculum decisions.

3. ISCED levels shown are only provided as a general indication, and do not represent ISCED reporting for Canada as a whole. Additionally, this information only reflects the formal public K-12 system for each.

Source: Data from the PQC, item 0.3

StatLink https://doi.org/10.1787/888934195758

Figure 7 [4/6] **Age coverage of curriculum frameworks across different levels of education**

This table captures the coverage of different curriculum frameworks by age band and ISCED level.

ISCED level 0	ISCED level 1	ISCED level 2	ISCED level 3	Overlap of age group
frameworks across multiple ISCED levels		not mandatory		

10 year-olds (11)	11 year-olds (12)	12 year-olds (13)	13 year-olds (14)	14 year-olds (15)	15 year-olds (16)	16 year-olds (17)	17 year-olds (18)	18 year-olds (19)	19 year-olds (20)		
7-15/16 year-olds (Basic Education Standard)							15/16 - 18/19 year-olds (Secondary Education Standard)			Latvia	OECD
7-10 year-olds (Primary)	11-16 year-olds (Lower Secondary)						17-18 year-olds (Upper Secondary)			Lithuania	
7-11 year-olds (Cycle 1 & 2 & 3)		12-14 year-olds		15-18 year-olds						Luxembourg	
		Enseignement Secondaire									
6-11 year-olds(National Elementary School Curriculum)		12-14 year-olds (National Middle School Curriculum)		15-17 year-olds (National High School Curriculum)						Korea	
6-11 year-olds (Primary)		12-15 year-olds (Secondary school)			15-18 year-olds					Mexico	
4-12 year-olds (doelen* Objectives)		12-15 year-olds			16-18 year-olds					Netherlands	
Curriculum and Te Marautanga o Aotearoa (the national curriculum for Māori medium schooling) up-18										New Zealand	
4-11 year-olds	11-14 year-olds		14-18 year-olds							Northern Ireland (United Kingdom)[1]	
6-12 year-olds (Kunnskapsløftet 2020 / Knowledge Promotion 2020)		13-15 year-olds (Kunnskapsløftet 2020 (KL20) / Knowledge Promotion 2020)			16-18 year-olds (Kunnskapsløftet 2020 (KL20) / Knowledge Promotion 2020)					Norway	
The Ontario Curriculum: Elementary		The Ontario Curriculum: Elementary, Grades 7 & 8, and The Ontario Curriculum: Secondary, Grades 9 & 10				The Ontario Curriculum: Secondary, Grades 11 & 12				Ontario (Canada)[3]	
7-15 year-olds						15-19 year-olds				Poland	
10-11 year-olds (2nd Cycle)	12-15 year-olds (3rd Cycle)				15-18 year-olds (Secondary)					Portugal	
Québec Education Program (QEP): Elementary	QEP: Secondary Cycle One		QEP: Secondary Cycle Two							Québec (Canada)[3]	
10-15 year-olds						16-18 year-olds				Sweden	
6-15 year-olds (Curriculum for the compulsory school, preschool class and school-age educare - revised 2018)											
Primary School (grades 1-4)				Secondary Schools (grades 9-12)						Turkey	
(m)										Wales (United Kingdom)	
										United States[1,2]	

Notes: Curriculum frameworks for the different ISCED levels (0 to 3) are shown as bars in increasingly darker shades of blue. Overlaps between different ISCED-level frameworks are marked in dark grey. The figure further depicts overarching curriculum frameworks reported by countries/jurisdictions that do not necessarily correspond to just one ISCED level, which are shown as white boxes with a black frame. Education levels that are non-mandatory are highlighted in light grey. Age brackets where there is no framework coverage are left blank.

1. Data submitted by researcher not governmental institution.

2. United States: Individual states determine their own curricula structure. In many states, local school districts make all curriculum decisions.

3. ISCED levels shown are only provided as a general indication, and do not represent ISCED reporting for Canada as a whole. Additionally, this information only reflects the formal public K-12 system for each.

Source: Data from the PQC, item 0.3

StatLink ᵇᵐˢ⌐ https://doi.org/10.1787/888934195758

Figure 7 [5/6] Age coverage of curriculum frameworks across different levels of education

This table captures the coverage of different curriculum frameworks by age band and ISCED level.

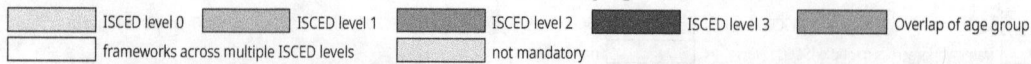

Legend: ISCED level 0 | ISCED level 1 | ISCED level 2 | ISCED level 3 | Overlap of age group | frameworks across multiple ISCED levels | not mandatory

Partner	0 year-olds (1)	1 year-olds (2)	2 year-olds (3)	3 year-olds (4)	4 year-olds (5)	5 year-olds (6)	6 year-olds (7)	7 year-olds (8)	8 year-olds (9)	9 year-olds (10)
Argentina										
Brazil[1]	0-3 year-olds (Creches) (not mandatory)				4-5 year-olds (Pré-Escolas)		6-10 year-olds (Fundamental I, grades 1-5)			
China (People's Republic of)							6-12 year-olds			
Hong Kong (China)				3-5 year-olds (Kindergarten Education)			6-11 year-olds (Primary Education)			
Costa Rica	Up-6 year-olds							6-12 year-olds		
India[1]							up to 6 year-olds	6-10 year-olds		
Kazakhstan				3-6 year-olds				6-11 year-olds		
Russian Federation	2mth-6 year-olds (Pre-school Educational Standard)							6-10 year-olds (Primary School Educational Standard)		
Singapore					Pre-primary (ISCED 0)			Primary (ISCED 1)		
South Africa	0-3 year-olds (Early Childhood Development)				4-5 year-olds (Grade R)		5-7 years-olds (Foundation phase)		8-10 year-olds (Intermediate)	
Viet Nam	3 months-5 year-olds (Nursery and Kindergarten)						6-10 years old (primary)			

Notes: Curriculum frameworks for the different ISCED levels (0 to 3) are shown as bars in increasingly darker shades of blue. Overlaps between different ISCED-level frameworks are marked in dark grey. The figure further depicts overarching curriculum frameworks reported by countries/jurisdictions that do not necessarily correspond to just one ISCED level, which are shown as white boxes with a black frame. Education levels that are non-mandatory are highlighted in light grey. Age brackets where there is no framework coverage are left blank.

1. Data submitted by researcher not governmental institution.

2. United States: Individual states determine their own curricula structure. In many states, local school districts make all curriculum decisions.

3. ISCED levels shown are only provided as a general indication, and do not represent ISCED reporting for Canada as a whole. Additionally, this information only reflects the formal public K-12 system for each.

Source: Data from the PQC, item 0.3

StatLink https://doi.org/10.1787/888934195758

Figure 7 [6/6] Age coverage of curriculum frameworks across different levels of education

This table captures the coverage of different curriculum frameworks by age band and ISCED level.

Legend: ISCED level 0 ▢ | ISCED level 1 ▢ | ISCED level 2 ▢ | ISCED level 3 ▢ | Overlap of age group ▢ | frameworks across multiple ISCED levels ▢ | not mandatory ▢

10 year-olds (11)	11 year-olds (12)	12 year-olds (13)	13 year-olds (14)	14 year-olds (15)	15 year-olds (16)	16 year-olds (17)	17 year-olds (18)	18 year-olds (19)	19 year-olds (20)	
										Argentina
6-10 year-olds (Fundamental I, grades 1-5)	11-14 year-olds (Fundamental II, grades 6-9)				Up to 17 year-olds (Ensino Médio)					Brazil[1]
6-12 year-olds		12-15 year-olds								China (People's Republic of)
6-11 year-olds (Primary Education)		12-14 year-olds (Junior Secondary Education)			15-17 year-olds (Senior Secondary Education)					Hong Kong (China)
6-12 year-olds		13-17 year-olds			15-18 year-olds					Costa Rica
6-10 year-olds										India[1]
6-11 year-olds	11-16 year-olds					16-18 year-olds				Kazakhstan
	10-15 year-olds (Basic General Educational Standard)				16-18 year-olds (Secondary General Educational Standard)					Russian Federation
Primary (ISCED 1)			Lower Secondary (ISCED2)		Upper Secondary (ISCED3)		-			Singapore
8-10 year-olds (Intermediate)	11-13/14 year-olds (Senior Phase)				15-18 year-olds (Further Education and Training)					South Africa
6-10 years old (primary)	11-14 year-olds (lower secondary)				15-17 year-olds (upper secondary)					Viet Nam

(Right margin label: Partner)

Notes: Curriculum frameworks for the different ISCED levels (0 to 3) are shown as bars in increasingly darker shades of blue. Overlaps between different ISCED-level frameworks are marked in dark grey. The figure further depicts overarching curriculum frameworks reported by countries/jurisdictions that do not necessarily correspond to just one ISCED level, which are shown as white boxes with a black frame. Education levels that are non-mandatory are highlighted in light grey. Age brackets where there is no framework coverage are left blank.

1. Data submitted by researcher not governmental institution.

2. United States: Individual states determine their own curricula structure. In many states, local school districts make all curriculum decisions.

3. ISCED levels shown are only provided as a general indication, and do not represent ISCED reporting for Canada as a whole. Additionally, this information only reflects the formal public K-12 system for each.

Source: Data from the PQC, item 0.3

StatLink ᐧᐧᐧ https://doi.org/10.1787/888934195758

Furthermore, some countries/jurisdictions, such as Denmark, Finland and Japan, recognise that learning starts at age 0 by extending the curriculum framework to cover the early years (Figure 7). This approach contributes further to ensuring alignment between school requirements and children's natural learning process and developmental stages. This way, the curriculum in early-childhood, primary and secondary education can be seen as a continuum to prepare students to navigate future challenges with a progressive approach.

As seen earlier, content overload refers to excessive content expected to be taught in a limited amount of time. The number of mandated instruction hours per school year therefore sets the limits within which content is to be taught. When there is too much content planned and insufficient time to teach everything, the quality of teaching may suffer, in the absence of strategic decisions about what to prioritise.

Quality of learning time and student well-being

Empirical evidence on the relationship between school instruction time and student achievement is inconclusive. Added instruction time has been found to provide more learning opportunities and to correlate with higher academic achievement (Rivkin and Schiman, 2015[60]; Huebener, Kuger and Marcus, 2017[61]; Andersen, Humlum and Nandrup, 2016[62]). Extra instruction time has also been shown to help lower-performing students to catch up with higher-performing students (Rivkin and Schiman, 2015[60]; Lavy, 2015[63]). However, more hours of instruction do not automatically translate into better scores and quality learning (Alexander, 2009[32]; FitzPatrick and O'Shea, 2013[28]; Alexander and Flutter, 2009[4]; OECD, 2014[64]).

Furthermore, a growing body of research suggests that the relationship between hours of learning and student performance is not linear (Cattaneo, Oggenfuss and Wolter, 2017[65]; Huebener, Kuger and Marcus, 2017[61]). The 2015 report of the OECD Programme for International Student Assessment (OECD, 2016[66]) also found that time spent on learning, both within and outside school instruction time, does not correlate to students' academic performance (Figure 8). Transferring uncovered curricular content to students' personal time as homework also has been reported to have a potentially negative impact on students' mental and physical health (Chraif and Anitei, 2012[67]).

Compromising students' well-being with excessive learning hours or excessive homework is also a common challenge when addressing curriculum overload (See "What types of challenges do countries/jurisdictions face in addressing curriculum overload, and what strategies do they use to address these challenges?"). This challenge needs to be balanced with the benefits of homework, such as the long-term development of children's motivation, strategies for coping with mistakes and setbacks and the time for children to develop positive beliefs about achievement (Bempchat, 2004[68]).

If teachers feel pressured to teach everything in an overloaded curriculum, it may also lead them to teach a shallow version of the curriculum or to leave what cannot be covered in school instruction time for students to pick up in their personal time outside of school. Content overload may also be further challenged by or may, in some instances, encourage the use of private tutors, also known as shadow education (Bray, 2011[69]). In Asia and parts of Europe, it is common for students to participate in tutoring after the school day, either as a supplement to their typical day or to help students with content from their school work. In Japan, for example, this is called *juku*, while in Korea, it is known as *hagwon*.

In some countries/jurisdictions that have undergone curriculum redesign or otherwise have an overloaded curriculum, parents sought out additional help when students could not finish the material. In Malta, for example, teachers expressed the need to finish the curriculum at all costs, even if students could not follow the material (Budiene and Zabulionis, 2006[70]). Elsewhere, the trend is for tutors to supplement with extra material, potentially dominating students' already burdened lives and contributing to adverse psychological and educational outcomes (Bukowski, 2017[71]). There is also a significant gap in use of tutoring services by socio-economic status, with higher-income families being more likely to use such services, again, contributing to educational disparities (Bray, 2020[72]).

Acknowledging that students are all different and they learn differently, including their prior knowledge and pace of learning, it is essential to anticipate the needs of teachers for guidance on priorities, as mentioned earlier. Teachers otherwise may attempt to cover everything for all students and some students, in particular low-performing students, may feel overwhelmed by the volume of content in any given learning unit. To meet expectations, they may need to spend a lot of extra time studying outside school hours on top of regular extra-curricular activities. This can make it difficult for them to participate in other activities that are important for full development and fostering a balanced lifestyle, such as time to socialise and be with friends, time to play, time to exercise and time to sleep (Marhefka, 2011[73]).

Student voice is critical in understanding overload as countries/jurisdictions seek to avoid it. Box 2 explores student perspectives on their educational experiences in relation to learning hours. In addition to learning within school, many participate in other activities and have other demands on their time. They report being busy and eager to be able to spend more time on topics that engage them.

Figure 8 Relationship between PISA scores and learning time

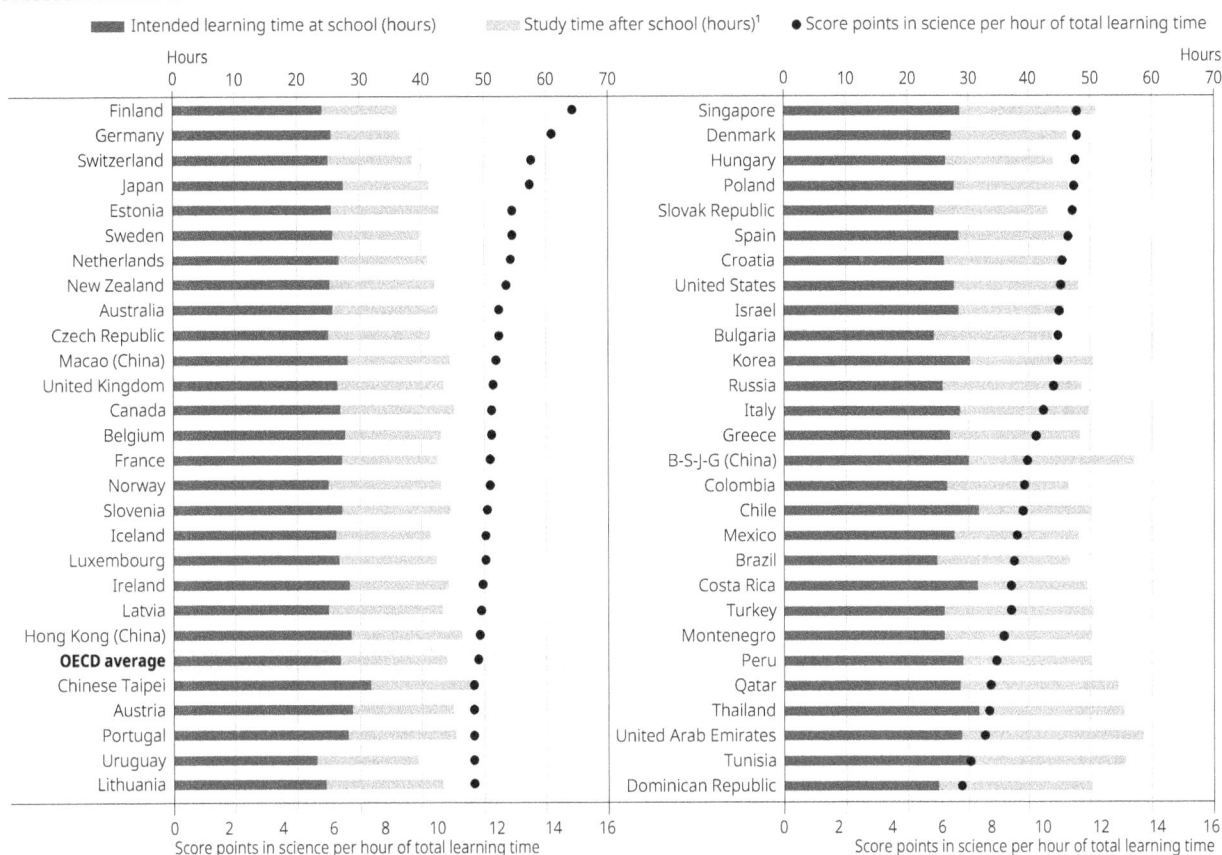

■ Intended learning time at school (hours)   ▦ Study time after school (hours)[1]   ● Score points in science per hour of total learning time

Note: 1. Hours spent learning in addition to the required school schedule, including homework, additional instruction and private study.

Countries and economies are ranked in descending order of the score points in science per hour of total learning time.

Source: OECD, PISA 2015 Database, Figure II.6.23, https://doi.org/10.1787/9789264267510-en.

StatLink ⁂ https://doi.org/10.1787/888934195777

Box 2 Student perspectives on curriculum overload

During the 9th Informal Working Group meeting (IWG) in British Columbia (Canada), students from the Education 2030 project's Focus Group 3 shared their perspectives on how their school schedules impact their learning and well-being and what changes could improve this relationship. Most students felt that their schedules were jam-packed with classes and study time. The majority of participating students had at least six hours of classes and two hours of self-study every day. Upon reflecting on the concept of deep learning, most students wished they had more time to dig deeper into topics that interest them or to engage in extra-curricular activities without compromising most of their free time.

Maria is a 16-year-old student from Portugal who likes her school but finds her schedule a bit too demanding: "I have too many classes, which does not help, because quantity does not mean quality. It makes me feel tired and lowers my school performance." Every day, she attends school from 8:30 until 17:30. On Fridays, she enjoys practicing sports after school, but on other weekdays she goes home to study until 21:00. She thinks that since not all time spent in school is always used productively, having fewer classes would improve her well-being without hampering her learning: "If school ended early, I would have more time to sign up for activities, for self-study and for group projects."

Ayumi is a 15-year-old student from Japan. She lives a bit far from school, so every day, she wakes up at 6:00 (earlier than she'd like to!) to commute there on a local train. During the Education 2030 IWG meeting in British Columbia, she realised that her school day is just as intense as that of many students in other countries. Every day, from 8:00 until 15:00, Ayumi has six 1-hour learning blocks. After this, she usually helps to clean her classroom and then stays at school to attend club activities. That semester, she signed up for swimming. When she gets home at 18:00, she has dinner with family and works on homework until 20:30. After this, during her free time, she sometimes reads books about historical figures before going to bed: "Sometimes I hear about interesting characters during history classes, and then I read about them at home. It would be interesting if we had time to talk more about them in school, but this is not always the case."

Jay is a 17-year-old student from British Columbia (Canada) who, on top of attending school, also works part-time. Her school day usually starts at 8:00 and goes until 13:30. She enjoys having no classes in the afternoon because it allows her to work, study, practice sports and spend time with her mother, who is ill. She thinks that she learns more when school classes have a good balance between teaching time and practice: "When teachers provide content on and on during classes I have a harder time paying attention. I find lessons where we have to solve problems more interesting. Some teachers would give us problems to work on at home and then we use in-class time to discuss different approaches of looking at these issues. However, because I work and take care of my mother, I prefer days when not all teachers send homework at the same time."

Teachers' sense of agency, professionalism and well-being

Excessive content may also require teachers to spend extra time outside of teaching hours to prepare lesson plans and assess students' progress, including grading and providing individual feedback to students. Furthermore, the "mile-wide-and-inch-deep" approach mentioned earlier can lead to disengagement among students and teachers. Some repetitions are deliberately built into a curriculum for students to reinforce and deepen their understanding of concepts or ideas that they are learning in a developmentally appropriate sequencing. However, topics that appear repeatedly within and across disciplines without a clear purpose are likely to create negative perceptions and experiences among students and teachers (Schmidt, Wang and McKnight, 2005[29]; Schmidt, Houang and Cogan, 2002[30]).

Teachers in countries/jurisdictions where their administrative load is already significant (which is not uncommon in Asian countries, such as Korea and Japan) may end up investing time outside of working hours to meet the expectations. Lesson preparation and administrative tasks related to the curriculum may reduce the time actually consecrated to teaching. If only a small amount of their time is actually spent teaching, teachers' sense of overload may further increase. Of their working time, they only spend an average of 53% on teaching (Figure 9).

Figure 9 **Weekly hours teachers report spending at school**

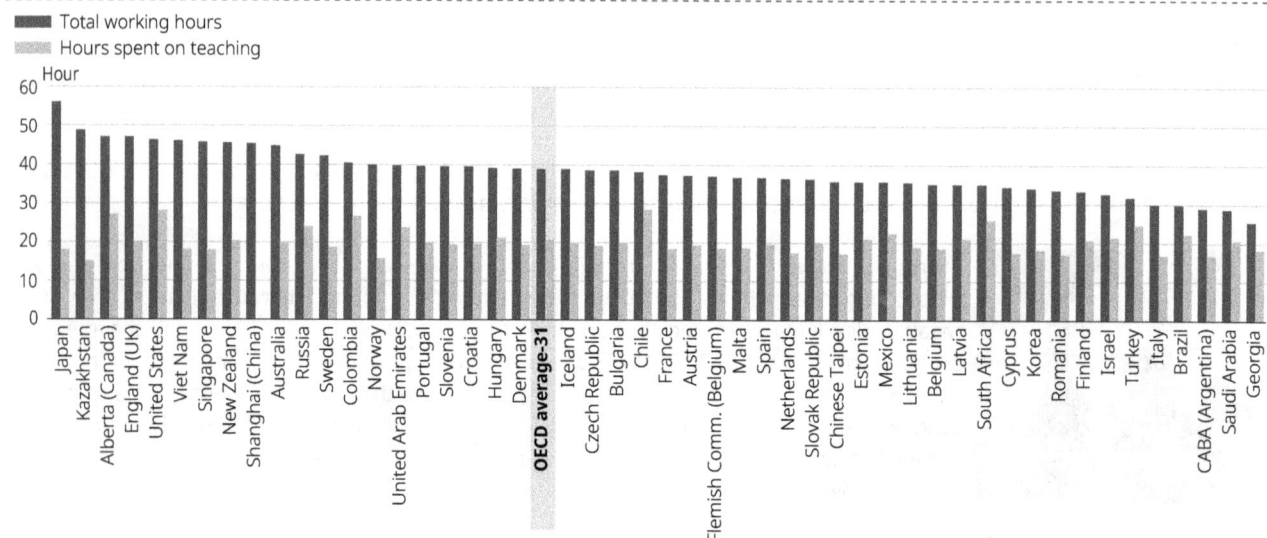

Note: Average number of 60-minute hours teachers report having spent at the current school on the following activities during the most recent complete calendar week. Countries and economies are ranked in descending order of the average number of total working hours of teachers.

Information on data for Cyprus: https://oe.cd/cyprus-disclaimer

Source: TALIS 2018 Results (Volume I), OECD 2019, Table I.4.57, https://doi.org/10.1787/1d0bc92a-en.

StatLink ᵐˢᵖ https://doi.org/10.1787/888934195796

An unsustainable workload is also associated with teachers' decisions to leave the profession (Torres, 2016[74]). In addition, the non-teaching-related workload of teachers or the time devoted to preparing lessons or performing administrative duties is strongly related to burnout, whereas teaching-related workload has a more modest relationship (Lawrence, Loi and Gudex, Teachers and Teaching[75]). The more responsibilities teachers have, the more time they will need to spend away from their core activity of teaching. For teachers to feel supported and remain in the profession, it may be critical to monitor the time they spend on their work outside of the classroom.

Curriculum overload can, therefore, threaten teachers' ability to cope with expectations, impact their levels of satisfaction with the profession and deprive them of their sense of agency by leaving no room for their own creativity. It can also affect their individual well-being, through chronic fatigue due to excessive working hours.

Pitch for what to include in a curriculum

Content overload is also caused when overly ambitious learning goals and student outcomes are set in a curriculum without careful consideration for the allotted space and time. Additional sources of content overload can arise based on how they are translated into syllabuses, textbooks, assessment materials and homework. A fundamental challenge for curriculum designers is to define the right "pitch" in the curriculum. This means achieving an appropriate level of aspirations, ambitions and challenges for all students while recognising the differences among students' learning progressions and their prior knowledge and skills. Content overload is thus a relative concept, as it depends on who uses the curriculum.

Neuroscience research confirms what many teachers already know from experience, that the brain can respond to stimuli and benefit more from learning if content and the learning environment are aligned for optimal stimulation and reinforcement (Dubinsky, Roehrig and Varma, 2013[76]). When students are bored or stressed (due to excessive demands, fear of failure and repeated information), their metabolic responses may block information from being processed in the brain, with clear negative implications for learning (Dubinsky, Roehrig and Varma, 2013[76]; Goswami, 2008[77]).

The challenges when defining the pitch for curriculum include trade-offs between aiming higher and focusing on essentials, and ensuring opportunities to learn and opportunities to succeed.

Trade-offs between aiming higher and focusing on essentials

A curriculum without high aspirations or challenging contents can lead to disengagement among high-performing students, while a curriculum with overly ambitious aspirations and too much content can risk disengagement among low-performing students, leaving them to fall behind. There is no silver bullet and no single answer to determine the right pitch for a curriculum that can capture the needs and aspirations of all students.

Japan, for example, reduced content and decreased the amount of instruction time in its 1998 reform to ease anxiety among students and parents about intensified competition for university entrance. The goal was to leave no student to fall behind and to enhance the quality of learning time, but the reform was misunderstood as a lowering of standards. In response to a backlash to that reform, the 2008 curriculum increased both content and instruction time.

Hong Kong (China) reported that the curriculum set at the high end of the standards was pitched for the full ability spectrum of students, but the curriculum allows adaptations to cater to the individual needs of students. Higher-ability students might cover all of the content, while lower-ability students may study only the foundational elements rather than all content. However, many schools and parents that were not accustomed to such an idea would encourage all students to study all content items. As a result, weaker students found that studying all of the curriculum content was too heavy (See "What types of challenges do countries/jurisdictions face in addressing curriculum overload, and what strategies do they use to address these challenges?").

When expectations are unrealistic, some teachers may decide to partially cover the content specified in the curriculum while assigning the remaining parts for students' self-learning through additional homework assignments. As noted earlier, this can have negative consequences for students' well-being.

Ensuring opportunities to learn and opportunities to succeed

When excessive content sets out unrealistic expectations, learning goals end up not being met as intended. In Chile, for example, research on the coverage of the curriculum reveal that a majority of courses offered in mathematics and language do not cover 100% of the minimum mandatory objectives (Ramírez, 2006[78]). If students will need literacy and numeracy as a prerequisite to learn new content in later grades, students whose teachers did not cover the previous contents are likely to miss out on opportunities to learn. The more fundamental concepts and skills these students miss, the higher the chances are that they will also miss out on opportunities to succeed, at in later stages in life. Therefore, core foundations should be considered as fundamental priorities in the curriculum.

Children from socio-economically disadvantaged backgrounds in particular may miss out on these key opportunities. Research from the United States has shown that poor reading skills of third-grade students, who do not have access to reading materials or opportunities to learn to read at home are associated with lower chances of students graduating from high school (Hernandez, 2011[79]; Sparks, 2020[80]). Such research findings reinforce the importance of public policies, including the purpose and function of a curriculum in addressing inequity.

When selecting what subjects/topics to include in a curriculum and in what order, it is important to consider each subject-specific learning goal as an independent block that should develop only in a linear sequential order, but rather as an inter-dependent piece of a puzzle which can help a student to learn. The piece then fits within and across different subjects in a developmentally appropriate sequential order. The sequence should consider the nature of each subject; some subjects require a linear and hierarchical order when learning concepts for the developmentally appropriate sequencing (e.g. mathematics) and others (e.g. history) do not assume sequential or hierarchical progression but learning is measured by mastery of levels of complexity within each skill, which can occur in a concurrent and interrelated manner (Zarmati, 2019[81]; Confrey, 2019[82]).

Education is a complex system with students in classrooms influenced by their teachers, schools, communities, local and regional educational agencies within states; all of which have an influence on the content, pedagogy, and outcomes as a part of a larger ecosystem. An ecosystem approach to curriculum design (see the Overview Brochure) is still new, and thus there is not yet a solid body of research. However, some countries/jurisdictions have started to explore this concept as a new form of spiral curriculum, as in Estonia, Ireland, and New Zealand (See "What types of challenges do countries/jurisdictions face in addressing curriculum overload, and what strategies do they use to address these challenges?").

The size, volume, and language of curriculum documents

Content overload may also be related to the excessive size of curriculum-setting statutory documents (i.e. the number of objectives, subjects and pages in which the curriculum is defined and elaborated) (Australian Primary Principals Association, 2014[10]; FitzPatrick and O'Shea, 2013[28]; Haug, 2003[26]; Voogt, Nieveen and Klopping, 2017[1]; ACARA, 2018[83]; NCCA, 2010[84]; Hong and Youngs, 2019[85]; Sousa, 2013[86])[8].

The number of pages and words in curriculum documents can indicate overload: "…it is a strong measure of general overcrowding such that, if teachers have to read a greater number of pages to understand the curriculum, they will take longer to understand what is expected of them" (Australian Primary Principals Association, 2014, p. 4[10])[9].

For example, the 1999 Irish primary school curriculum content was elaborated in 23 books amounting to over 3 650 pages (FitzPatrick and O'Shea, 2013, p.126[28]). As of 2014, Australia's curriculum comprised over 1 700 pages (Australian Primary Principals Association, 2014[10])[10]. This rendered the curriculum difficult to understand and manage, with teachers struggling to divide instruction time to cover all subjects while trying to meet the needs of all students (FitzPatrick and O'Shea, 2013[28]).

Some countries/jurisdictions have been able to appropriately adjust their curriculum. Norway reduced the volume of curriculum documents, used clearer language, and made priorities clearer when reducing content. On the other hand, Ontario (Canada) experienced a distinct challenge. Although the size of the mandatory curriculum itself was short, teachers did not consistently make a distinction between the core curriculum and optional guidelines. That led to the misunderstanding that there was more content to teach than what was actually in the mandatory document (See "What types of challenges do countries/jurisdictions face in addressing curriculum overload, and what strategies do they use to address these challenges?").

Another experience commonly reported by several countries/jurisdictions is that, even when a national curriculum can be stated in a short, concise form, the brief form can actually create overload and incoherence at the school level. Perceived overload is mainly due to a lack of specific details and clarity on what should be taught and to what depth and the task of developing a working curriculum at local and school levels. Uncertainty, anxiety and ineffectiveness all can be high, especially for teachers, when there is much local political pressure without proper support mechanisms (Kyriacou, 2011[87]).

WHAT IS PERCEIVED OVERLOAD? HOW DOES IT AFFECT STUDENTS AND TEACHERS?

Excessive content is also measured based on end-user feedback from teachers, administrators and students (Kuiper, Nieveen and Berkvens, 2013[6]; Silver et al., 2011[88]). Thus, it is critically important to distinguish between actual and perceived overload. Policy makers first need to establish facts, by asking such questions as:

- Is overload "real" or "perceived"? (as discussed in the section above on content overload)

- If the overload is real, what factors might explain it?

- If the overload is a perceived, whose perception is it? And what are the possible sources or roots of such a perception?

If the overload is real, one possible solution is to reduce content, as in Korea, Norway and Singapore. If the overload is real, with a dilemma in trade-offs between schools and national authorities in responsibility for curriculum design, as in Finland, Norway, and New Zealand, the country-specific context affecting that balance must be addressed.

If the overload is a perception, different solutions are possible, depending on the country-specific context. For example, it was necessary to address assessment overload in Australia[11], mistrust in frequent curriculum changes in Japan, and misunderstanding about focusing on essentials and lowering standards in Portugal.

Once perceived overload is identified as an issue, policy makers can consider ways to strategically manage stakeholders' perceptions. In curriculum redesign processes, it is of critical importance to anticipate and manage potential unintended processes and consequences. For example, the National Council for Curriculum and Assessment in Ireland suggests perceptions of overload as follows:

> Much of what we know about curriculum overload comes from teachers. Some observers may question the extent to which the overload phenomenon is imagined, perceived or real. (…) National and international experience and evidence (…) suggests that the overload issue is very much a reality for teachers, and paradoxically, is often an unintended consequence of education reform." (NCCA, 2010, p. 7[27]).

In fact, curriculum overload is an intricately intertwined mix of reality and perception. To reduce the risk of unintended consequences, it is very valuable to learn more about possible consequences through both research and the experience of peer countries/jurisdictions. The main factors driving perceived overload include: the number of subjects/topics to cover in the allotted time; the frequency, focus and types of assessments, textbooks, learning materials and homework; the size and volume of curriculum documents; the structure and coherence of the curriculum; and the lack of readiness for reform or reform fatigue.

Perception driven by the number of subjects/topics to cover in the allotted time

Too many subjects/topics to teach within a specific time frame can cause actual content overload, but it also be a question of perception. Based on end-user feedback, teachers' perceptions of having "too much to teach" within the available instruction time can be one of the main criteria for identifying curriculum content overload (Australian Primary Principals Association, 2014[10])[12]. Finland sees overload stemming from this too, citing criticism from teachers that its previous National Core Curriculum had more to do with "heaviness" created at the local level than requirements outlined in the national document (See "What types of challenges do countries face in addressing curriculum overload, and what strategies do they use to address these challenges?").

Teachers who perceive that there are too many topics in their subject curriculum may feel pressured to provide extensive coverage of the content required by the curriculum. This perception may lead to shallow rather than deeper learning for students. This, in turn, may frustrate teachers and sap their motivation and sense of purpose, i.e. teacher agency, as described in the OECD Learning Compass 2030 (OECD, 2019[14]). Ultimately, they may be unable to exercise professional judgment.

On the other hand, teachers may make individual decisions on what they can realistically teach within a given learning unit or cycle. This could result in discrepancies in the taught curriculum across classrooms and schools and even the entire system.

Perception driven by the frequency, focus and types of assessments

Perceptions about content overload are also driven by a sense of assessment overload. As students do not read the learning goals in the written curriculum document itself, they are most likely to perceive or experience examinations and assessments as the most visible learning goals. Indeed, students often only see assessments as the curriculum (Ramsden, 1993[89]). Assessments drive what students perceive as being important to learn (Brown, Bull and Pendlebury, 2013[90]) and what is eventually retained in a curriculum across redevelopment cycles (Kärkkäinen, 2012[91]).

Although the curriculum may encourage development of more holistic skills alongside content knowledge, when exams are heavily based on mastering content, students will likely be steered towards what gets tested at the expense of other important development areas. This "teaching to the test" can mean that what could be mastered will be compromised by what will be tested (Jennings and Bearak, 2014[92]). This phenomenon is more commonly seen at the high school level as students approach their transition to college, but it can also be observed in early grades.

The types of assessments matter as well. Reliance on examinations, particularly high-stakes exams to pass to another grade or for college entrance, can cause significant anxiety, as early as in primary school (Segool et al., 2013[93]). Moreover, test anxiety decreases performance in school (McDonald, 2010[94]). Depth of learning and retention may also not be as great as that achieved through other forms of assessments or engagement with learning material (Hackthorn et al., 2011[95]). When curriculum relies on exams, especially as the sole assessment technique or as a gatekeeping tool, students' well-being can suffer.

Finally, curriculum standards and assessment must be aligned. Without clear progression and scaffolding of the curriculum, students may struggle to learn (Heritage, 2008[96]). Having the time and opportunity to learn could be further challenged in an overloaded curriculum.

Perception driven by the size of curriculum documents, textbooks, learning materials and homework

The size, volume and details of a curriculum can cause actual content overload, as discussed earlier, but they can also create the perception or the experience of overload among students, teachers and principals (Voogt, Nieveen and Klopping, 2017[1]).

Students are unlikely to know much about the sheer volume of the physical curriculum and related documents, but they can be a burden for teachers. At each cycle of education reform and curriculum redesign, an excessive number of pages in new curriculum documents may signal to teachers that the curriculum is overloaded. An immediate negative reaction to very large documents may set the scene for a perception of curriculum overload, even if the curriculum avoids an overly prescriptive tone and is careful to include detailed guidance to teachers on how to implement it (See "What types of challenges do countries/jurisdictions face in addressing curriculum overload, and what strategies do they use to address these challenges?").

Perceptions about curriculum overload are also created by excessive use of textbooks, learning materials and homework. For example, too much homework that is not explained well or does not have clear links to course material, can be boring, demotivating, and ineffective in helping learning (Bryan and Burstein, 2004[97]). The content and volume of textbooks can also be excessive and not appropriately modified to a new curriculum or local contexts and culture (Wang, 2014[98]). This makes them difficult for teachers to use and overwhelming for students and parents. Textbooks can have a cultural bias too, making them less accessible to all learners (Wang, 2014[98]; Ndura, 2004[99]). Easy-to-use teaching materials can also help ensure that a curriculum is implemented as intended and reduce teacher frustration (Kärkkäinen, 2012[91]).

Curriculum documents should support teachers to effectively convey and support the curriculum and learning by their students. Similarly, textbooks should be a resource for students to reinforce learning in the classroom and convey material clearly. However, when the curriculum is overloaded or textbooks are not appropriately modified, teachers can be frustrated and students overwhelmed.

Perception driven by the lack of readiness for reform or reform fatigue

Teachers' perceptions on curriculum change in general may accelerate or alleviate their perceptions on content overload. They are not always ready for reform. Finland reported that teachers involved in developing curricula tend to add rather than replace content, observing that they want to add new content in response to changing times and needs, but they hardly let go of any of the previous goals or content[13]. This suggests that teachers may perceive content overload differently depending on their own preparedness for curriculum change and readiness to digest and use any new support materials.

Busy teachers may not find the time to review such long documents and fully understand the new curriculum. They may become dismissive of the latest reform, preferring instead to resort to their previous classroom practices and lesson plans as something more feasible and long-standing. They may quickly lose interest in better understanding the new curriculum and discount it as one more transitory reform cycle that is likely to be short-lived. These are some signs of reform fatigue among teachers that can be sparked simply by the physical presentation of the curriculum (Dilkes, 2014[100]). However, mechanisms and processes can be put in place to effectively manage change and provide additional support and coaching to teachers and administrators (see "What types of challenges do countries/jurisdictions face in addressing curriculum overload, and what strategies do they use to address these challenges? ").

WHAT IS CURRICULUM IMBALANCE? HOW DOES IT AFFECT STUDENTS AND TEACHERS?

Curriculum imbalance occurs when certain subjects are given priority at the expense of others. More precisely, it refers to disproportionate attention given to certain portions of a curriculum at the expense of others without corresponding adjustments in the conditions or expectations for teaching and learning in those low priority areas. Such imbalance creates a sense of overload in prioritised subjects and a sense of being under-valued or threatened by competition with other subjects. Given that curriculum space is limited, any curriculum choices imply trade-offs.

Some countries/jurisdictions make a distinction between core and non-core subjects. In many OECD countries and partner economies, this usually corresponds to a distinction between academic and non-academic subjects (Table 4). To a lesser extent, some countries/jurisdictions intentionally avoid making the distinction, according the same priority to academic and non-academic subjects, as in British Columbia (Canada), Ontario (Canada) and Québec (Canada), Chile, the Czech Republic, New Zealand, Portugal and Sweden, as well as in partner countries like Argentina, China and India.

Table 4 **Distinction between core and non-core subjects in the curriculum**

Makes the distinction		No distinction	
OECD	Partner	OECD	Partner
Australia	Brazil[1]	British Columbia (Canada)	Argentina
Denmark	Hong Kong (China)	Chile	China
Estonia	Costa Rica	Czech Republic	India[1]
Hungary	Kazakhstan	Finland	
Ireland	Russian Federation	New Zealand	
Japan[2]	South Africa	Ontario (Canada)	
Korea		Portugal	
Lithuania		Québec (Canada)	
Netherlands		Scotland (United Kingdom)	
Northern Ireland (United Kingdom)[1]		Sweden	
Norway			
Poland			
Turkey			
United States[1]			

Note: Values displayed in this table include only countries/jurisdictions with responses that could be clearly coded as yes/no.

1. Responses for these countries/jurisdictions were submitted by independent researchers, not government administrations.

2. Japan makes the distinction in upper secondary education, but not in elementary and lower secondary education.

Source: Data from the PQC, item 1.1.3.2.

Portugal abandoned the distinction between core and non-core subjects in 2016. This distinction had been introduced in 2012 to harmonise curricula on a national level, but teachers and families considered it too restrictive. New Zealand does not use this distinction either, but uses other measures to indicate the relative importance of learning, such as the introduction of national standards for literacy and mathematics.

Such priority subjects are often given a disproportionate amount of instruction time (NCCA, 2010[27]). Such decisions are often driven by the social and political agenda, high-stakes national or state examinations, and/or international assessments.

Social and political agenda

Over-prioritisation of some subjects may occur by the force of tradition, often for elements considered as "core curriculum" or "the basics" that are historically seen as most important within the school curriculum. It can also occur when the curriculum becomes a means for delivering certain social and political agendas. The United States and European countries sought to strengthen their mathematics and science curriculum as an avenue to boost their international competitiveness (Sahlberg, 2016[101]). Many countries in Africa revised their curriculum to depart from the legacy of colonisation (Majoni, 2017[2]). Similarly, after the fall of Soviet Union, curriculum that had been heavily influenced by ideology was revised to strengthen national elements and develop a standards-based, skill-centred and outcome-oriented curriculum (Moreno, 2007[38]).

Reprioritisation of underprioritised subjects

When curriculum elements are prioritised or reprioritised without sufficient consideration of what content should be removed or replaced, the curriculum can lose its overall balance (ACARA, 2018[83]; Alexander and Flutter, 2009[4]; Kuiper, Nieveen and Berkvens, 2013[6]; van Silfhout, 2016[102]; Voogt, Nieveen and Klopping, 2017[1]). As school instruction time is limited, other subjects consequently receive less instruction time. For example, subjects such as physical education, arts and music often need to compete for instruction time with so-called "academic subjects" or with core subjects for space in the curriculum.

In Ireland, physical education was once perceived as an underprioritised subject in lower secondary education (MacPhail and Halbert, 2005[103]). This imbalance was addressed and physical education is now part of the core curriculum area of well-being in the Junior Cycle Reform 2015 (Ireland's reform of ISCED 2). All students must receive 135 hours of physical education spread across the three years. While there is no one-size-fits-all solution that applies across contexts, learning areas and grade levels, some approaches to curriculum content redesign do take into account the need to pre-emptively reduce the threat of content overload.

High-stakes national or state examinations

Over-prioritisation of some subjects and topics can be impacted by policy mechanisms, such as accountability systems and assessments, which signal subject priorities, especially when accountability mechanisms do not coherently link to the curriculum (Jennings and Bearak, 2014[92]). When there is a policy of high-stakes examinations and assessment of student performance (e.g. standardised testing, high school graduation exams, university entrance exams), curriculum may opt to allocate more instruction time to the subjects included in these high-stakes exams.

In England, amidst the focus on high-stakes testing and performance statistics, little or no resources (including instruction time) were allocated to arts and music education, despite the rhetorical commitment of the government of the time to foster creativity (Alexander and Flutter, 2009[4]). Traditionally, literacy and numeracy occupied half of the instruction time in England, while all other subjects had to be squeezed into the remaining half (Alexander, 2009[32]), as cited in (Voogt, Nieveen and Klopping, 2017[1]).

High-stakes examinations play an important role in determining how teachers set their priorities when balancing breadth and depth in curriculum content. Teachers may opt to use a teach-to-the-test approach in the subjects with high-stakes exams, although teachers in various contexts reportedly favour the breadth-of-learning approach, as it provides more curricular coherence and ensures coverage of the knowledge field (Schunk and Dibenedettto, 2016[56]). Teachers overwhelmed by requirements to cover an overloaded curriculum may, in turn, teach to the test, whereby subjects and learning items that are tested receive disproportionately more classroom attention.

Teachers who emphasise fast-paced content coverage may thus curtail in-depth reflection among students and discourage exploration of and engagement with curriculum content (Muijs and Reynolds, 2017[104]). High volumes of content to learn in a limited time may also lead to poor study habits that favour rote learning and memorisation rather than deep understanding, and the broader contexts of support matter for how children can learn and succeed in those contexts (Darling-Hammond et al., 2020[105]).

Furthermore, it has been reported that the teaching-to-the-test mode of instruction undermines teacher autonomy, restricts teachers' choice of pedagogical practices and limits instructional formats to repetition, rote learning and drill (van der Embse et al., 2017[106]). Teachers restricted to using the transmission model of teaching may experience loss of their agency to make professional decisions, choose pedagogies that work best for their students, foster critical thinking and creative group work, and apply content knowledge to everyday life (Stein, Kintz and Miness, 2016[107]). Narrowing of the role of teachers to fast-paced content delivery may deter potentially good candidates from joining the profession.

Even in countries whose curriculum places student well-being as part of their core values and goals, such high-stakes exams can increase levels of student anxiety and fear of failure (e.g. poor grades, not passing a test), thus negatively impacting their overall sense of life satisfaction. PISA data highlights the prevalence of school-related anxiety among 15-year-old students across OECD countries (Figure 10). This suggests the critical importance of a well-thought alignment between curriculum goals and assessment policies and practices (OECD, Forthcoming[108]).

The role of international assessments

Globalisation and international competitiveness have been highlighted as major rationales for prioritising literacy and numeracy as they are consistently and reliably measured by international student assessments, such as PISA, the International Association for the Evaluation of Educational Achievement's Progress in International Reading Literacy Study or its Trends in International Mathematics and Science Study. Recent changes to international assessments like PISA are integrating new innovative domains, such as collaborative problem solving, creative thinking or global competency; which help to expand the common understanding of what matters in learning (OECD, 2020[109]). (See "Local and global citizenship, peace").

However, international assessments do not always suggest narrowing of the curriculum. In Japan, a 1998 decision to reduce curriculum content had to be reversed to some extent in response to public concerns that schools were lowering the standards in public education. Those concerns were raised in light of the lower-than-expected results of Japanese students in the 2003 PISA study. Other countries/jurisdictions, including Ontario (Canada) (Sahlberg, 2016[101]) and the Netherlands (Kuiper, Nieveen and Berkvens, 2013[6]), opted to increase instructional time for those core subjects to better prepare students for national/provincial and international tests. For the same reasons, the 2002-15 No Child Left Behind legislation in the United States prompted most school districts to shift teaching time from social studies, arts and music to reading skills, mathematics and science (Sahlberg, 2016[101]). In analysing the impact of reform efforts on schooling, Pasi Sahlberg (2016[101]) concludes that: "Reading, mathematics and science have now become the main determinants of perceived success or failure of pupils, teachers, and schools in many education systems."

Regardless of overall curriculum requirements, implementation becomes a factor. Both teachers and students may experience curriculum imbalance and thus overload if the priority for teaching and learning is steered towards giving greater instructional time to some subjects at the expense of others (Lambert, 2001[110]). Thus, it is becoming increasingly important that school leaders and teachers become aware of the issue of curriculum overload themselves and can make informed curriculum decisions and choices as co-designers of an enacted curriculum.

Figure 10 **Prevalence of schoolwork-related anxiety, by gender**

Percentage of students who reported that they "agree" or "strongly agree" with the following statements

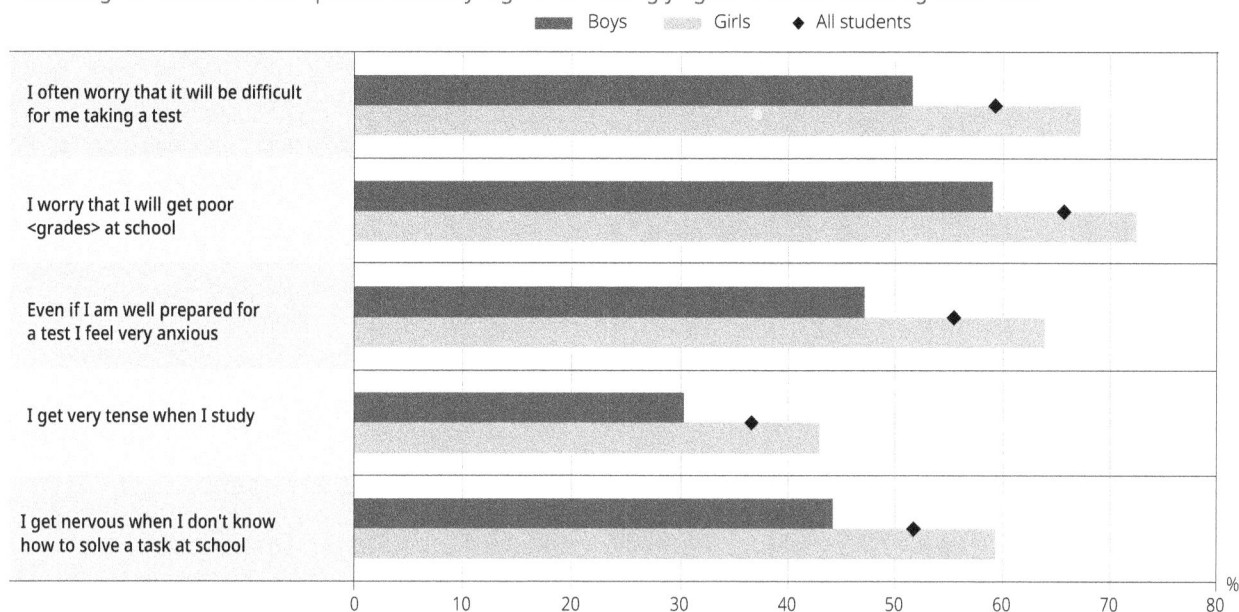

Source: OECD, PISA 2015 Database, Tables III.4.1, III.4.2 and III.4.5.
StatLink ᴍ⬛ https://dx.doi.org/10.1787/888933470845

WHAT IS STILL UNKNOWN?

Curriculum redesign occurs on regular intervals. This chapter has covered issues related to curriculum overload that policy makers can keep in mind when redesigning curriculum. Research has examined how overload can occur and suggested strategies and processes for designing curriculum with relevant stakeholders, being responsive to the needs and well-being of students. However, additional research can help illuminate how curriculum overload can be avoided and what components matter especially for students.

In general, there is limited research on curriculum overload. Research focused specifically on students is particularly lacking. Quantitative methodologies that can identify more precise links between curriculum in general and overload in particular are also lacking. Finally, the field can also benefit from additional research in more countries and jurisdictions.

A better understanding of curriculum overload can emerge as new research is conducted. Currently, much remains to be explored. Critical research needs include:

- **Research on this as a key policy issue**: Curriculum overload needs to be recognised as a policy research topic in its own right, not merely a consequence of misinformed education policy or a reason for failures in reform implementation. This includes the need to:

  - clarify the links between perceived and actual overload, fine-tune its definition and manifestations and explore in more detail the factors that contribute to it

  - examine the balance between coverage and depth of content that should be covered in curriculum, with more granular analysis of students of various socio-economic backgrounds and differing prior knowledge and skills among other factors

- accelerate research on political economy of reform with a specific focus on curriculum overload, as curriculum change is politically charged and has trade-offs in terms of policy solutions, with high costs for action or inaction.

- **Studies on student voices, choice and experiences**: Most existing research is focused on the perspectives of teachers, administrators and institutions, while the impact of curriculum overload on students remains under-researched (Schmidt and Houang, 2012[33]). There are very few studies documenting students' views and experiences on the number of topics covered in school. Research is also still scarce on student choice in the specific context of curriculum overload and content reduction is also still scarce (OECD, Forthcoming[111]).

- **Empirical studies involving quantitative methodologies**: Most of the available literature draws on qualitative methodologies and self-reporting techniques. While curriculum overload has a strong perceived dimension, impact studies are needed to identify the significance of various contributing factors and the relationships between them. This would make it possible to assess the effects of curriculum overload in the following ways:

  - By identifying the interplay of curriculum overload with related factors. It has been suggested that, instead of considering breadth and depth of a curriculum, attention should be paid to the balance between content and the learning process built into curricula, as well as to quantitative links between instruction time, academic performance, the quality of teaching and the type of student/school (Schwartz et al., 2009[36]).

  - By examining the effects of overload on students (learning outcomes and their well-being, in particular those of disadvantaged students); teachers (teaching practices, self-efficacy and teachers' well-being); parents (supporting students at home, e.g. homework overload issue, particularly for disadvantaged students), and the interplay among students, teachers and parents.

  - By investigating instructional time as a mediating factor of the effects of overload on students' learning outcomes, including the organisation of instruction time and its interplay with out-of-classroom activities (out-of-school schedule, sleep, play and socialisation).

  - By documenting curriculum coverage through empirical studies. Systematic school, local, regional and country data about how much of the curriculum is actually covered in schools can be very helpful for gauging levels of curriculum overload in various contexts.

- In-depth case studies from a greater number of regions and contexts: Available evidence-based literature is often limited to country-specific contexts, such as Australia, England (United Kingdom), Estonia, Ireland, the Netherlands, New Zealand and Singapore. Additional comparative research can identify contextual conditions of curriculum overload and effective solutions across educational contexts (e.g. federal and decentralised governments, tracking and non-tracking, and integrated and differentiated models of instruction).

Notes

1. Note concerning the current and subsequent references to Australian Primary Principals Association (APPA) in this report: The APPA views were written while the Australian Curriculum was being externally reviewed in 2014 and content overload was identified as an issue at that time.

2. See Note 1

3. See Note 1

4. Other compulsory curriculum includes different subjects that cannot be classified within the other groups or which specifically reflect national concerns. The following types of subjects could be included in this category: Latin, ancient Greek, classical studies, minority languages that have not been reported in the Languages 2-5 columns, environmental education, and personal development and well-being (OECD, 2018[143]). An in-depth analysis of other subjects included under "other" compulsory curriculum can be found in OECD subject-specific reports with an exclusive focus on domains like physical education (OECD, 2019[112]).

5. See Note 1

6. https://www.oecd.org/education/2030-project/contact/Conceptual_learning_framework_Conceptual_papers.pdf

7. See (OECD, 2020), *Overview brochure of the Education 2030 series of thematic reports on curriculum redesign*, OECD Publishing, Paris.

8. See Note 1

9. See Note 1

10. See Note 1

11. See Note 1

12. See Note 1

13. *OECD Future of Education and Skills 2030 Curriculum analysis*, Progress Report of 9th IWG meeting, [EDU/EDPC(2019)13/ANN1].

References

Abiko, T. (2019), 私教育再生 [Regeneration of private education], Sayusha.   [15]

Abiko, T. (ed.) (2008), 平成20年版　中学校新教育課程：教科・領域の改訂解説 [The new curriculum of lower secondary education in 2008:   [22]
commentary on revised subjects and areas of learning], Meijitosho.

ACARA (2018), *Monitoring the effectiveness of the foundation - Year 10 Australian curriculum*,   [83]
https://www.acara.edu.au/docs/default-source/curriculum/2018-monitoring-the-effectiveness-of-f-y10-australian-curriculum-report.pdf.

Aitken, G. (2005), *Curriculum design in New Zealand social studies: Learning from the past*, http://hdl.handle.net/2292/22856.   [24]

Alexander, R. (ed.) (2009), *Towards a new primary curriculum: A report from the Cambridge Primary Review. Part 2:The Future*, Cambridge   [32]
Primary Review.

Alexander, R. and J. Flutter (2009), *Towards a new primary curriculum. Part 1: Past and present*, Cambridge Primary Review, Cambridge,   [4]
http://dx.doi.org/10.13140/RG.2.1.3460.0086.

Ames, C. and R. Ames (eds.) (1989), *Stage-environment fit: Developmentally appropriate classrooms for young adolescents*, Academic Press.   [16]

Andersen, S., M. Humlum and A. Nandrup (2016), "Increasing instruction time in school does increase learning", *Proceedings of the*   [62]
National Academy of Sciences, Vol. 113/27, pp. 7481-7484, http://dx.doi.org/10.1073/pnas.1516686113.

Australian Primary Principals Association (2014), *The overcrowded primary curriculum: A way forward*,   [10]
https://www.appa.asn.au/wp-content/uploads/2015/08/Overcrowded-primary-curriculum.pdf.

Bempchat, J. (2004), "The Motivational Benefits of Homework: A Social-Cognitive Perspective", *Theory into practice*, Vol. 43/3, pp. 189-196,   [68]
http://dx.doi.org/10.1207/s15430421tip4303_4.

Boersma, K. (2001), *SLO en overladen onderwijs [SLO and overloaded education]*, SLO.   [23]

Brand, B. and C. Triplett (2012), "Interdisciplinary curriculum: An abandoned concept?", *Teachers and Learning: Theory and Practice*,   [46]
Vol. 18, pp. 381-393.

Bray, M. (2020), "Shadow Education in Europe: Growing Prevalence, Underlying Forces, and Policy Implications", *ECNU Review of Education*,   [72]
http://dx.doi.org/doi.org/10.1177/2096531119890142.

Bray, M. (2011), *The challenge of shadow education: Private tutoring and its implications for policy makers in the European Union*, European   [69]
Commission, Brussels.

Brown, G., J. Bull and M. Pendlebury (2013), *Assessing student learning in higher education*, Routledge.   [90]

Bruner, J. (1960), *The process of education*, Harvard University Press, Cambridge.   [21]

Bryan, T. and K. Burstein (2004), "Improving homework completion and academic performance: Lessons from special education", *Theory into Practice*, Vol. 43/3, pp. 213-219.   [97]

Bukowski, P. (2017), *Shadow education within the European Union from the perspective of investment in education*, London School of Economics, London, https://doi.org/10.1177/2096531119890142.   [71]

Cattaneo, M., C. Oggenfuss and S. Wolter (2017), "The More, the Better? The Impact of Instructional Time on Student Performance", *Education Economics*, Vol. 25/5, pp. 433-445, http://dx.doi.org/10.1080/09645292.2017.1315055.   [65]

Chraif, M. and M. Anitei (2012), "Overload Learning, Attachment and Coping Styles Predictors of Mental and Physical Health of Teenage High School Students in Romania", *Procedia - Social and Behavioral Sciences*, Vol. 69, pp. 1842-1846, http://dx.doi.org/10.1016/j.sbspro.2012.12.135.   [67]

Coker, J. et al. (2016), "Impacts of Experiential Learning Depth and Breadth on Student Outcomes", *Journal of Experiential Education*, Vol. 40/1, pp. 5-23, http://dx.doi.org/10.1177/1053825916678265.   [35]

Confrey, J. (2019), *Future of Education and Skills 2030: Curriculum analysis. A Synthesis of Research on Learning Trajectories/Progressions in Mathematics*, https://www.oecd.org/education/2030-project/about/documents/A_Synthesis_of_Research_on_Learning_Trajectories_Progressions_in_Mathematics.pdf.   [82]

Confrey, J. (2019), "Leading a Design-Based Research Team Using Agile Methodologies to Build Learner-Centered Software", in *Research in Mathematics Education, Designing, Conducting, and Publishing Quality Research in Mathematics Education*, Springer International Publishing, Cham, http://dx.doi.org/10.1007/978-3-030-23505-5_9.   [55]

Darling-Hammond, L. et al. (2020), "Implications for educational practice of the science of learning and development", *Applied Developmental Science*, Vol. 24/2, https://doi.org/10.1080/10888691.2018.1537791.   [105]

Department of Education and Skills (2015), *Framework for junior cycle 2015*, http://www.education.ie/en/Publications/Policy-Reports/Framework-for-Junior-Cycle-2015.pdf.   [17]

Dilkes, J. (2014), "The New Australian Curriculum, Teachers and Change Fatigue", *Australian Journal of Teacher Education*, Vol. 39/11, http://dx.doi.org/10.14221/ajte.2014v39n11.4.   [100]

Dubinsky, J., G. Roehrig and S. Varma (2013), "Infusing Neuroscience Into Teacher Professional Development", *Educational Researcher*, Vol. 42/6, pp. 317-329, http://dx.doi.org/10.3102/0013189x13499403.   [76]

Easthope, C. and G. Easthope (2000), "Intensification, Extension and Complexity of Teachers' Workload", *British Journal of Sociology of Education*, Vol. 21/1, pp. 43-58, http://dx.doi.org/10.1080/01425690095153.   [3]

European Commission (2018), *Council Recommendation of 22 May 2018 on key competences for lifelong learning (Text with EEA relevance.)*, pp. 1–13, https://eur-lex.europa.eu/legal-content/EN/TXT/?uri=uriserv%3AOJ.C_.2018.189.01.0001.01.ENG.   [8]

Fraser, K. et al. (2012), "Emotion, cognitive load and learning outcomes during simulation training", *Medical Education*, Vol. 46/11, pp. 1055-1062, https://doi.org/10.1111/j.1365-2923.2012.04355.x.   [31]

Giedd, J. (2004), "Structural Magnetic Resonance Imaging of the Adolescent Brain", *Annals of the New York Academy of Sciences*, Vol. 1021/1, pp. 77-85, http://dx.doi.org/10.1196/annals.1308.009.   [54]

Goswami, U. (ed.) (2008), *Principles of Learning, Implications for Teaching: A Cognitive Neuroscience Perspective*, Blackwell Publishing, Oxford, pp. 381-399, https://doi.org/10.1111/j.1467-9752.2008.00639.x.   [77]

Hackthorn, J. et al. (2011), "Learning by Doing: An Empirical Study of Active Teaching Techniques", *Journal of Effective Teaching*, Vol. 11/2, pp. 40-54.   [95]

Haug, P. (2003), *Evaluering av Reform 97: Sluttrapport frå styret for Program for evaluering av Reform 97 [Evaluation of Reform 97: Final report from the board of the Program for evaluation of Reform 97]*, Norges forskningsråd, Oslo, https://www.forskningsradet.no/siteassets/publikasjoner/1108644083551.pdf.   [26]

Heritage, M. (2008), *Learning progressions: Supporting instruction and formative assessment*, Council of Chief State School Officers, Washington, DC, https://csaa.wested.org/wp-content/uploads/2020/01/Learning_Progressions_Supporting_2008.pdf.   [96]

Hernandez, D. (2011), *Double jeopardy: How third-grade reading skills and poverty influence high school graduation*, https://files.eric.ed.gov/fulltext/ED518818.pdf.   [79]

Hong, W. and P. Youngs (2019), "Why are teachers afraid of curricular autonomy? Contradictory effects of the new national curriculum in South Korea", in *Teachers' Perceptions, Experience and Learning*, Routledge, http://dx.doi.org/10.4324/9781351173285-2.   [85]

Huebener, M., S. Kuger and J. Marcus (2017), "Increased instruction hours and the widening gap in student performance", *Labour Economics,* Vol. 47, pp. 15-34, http://dx.doi.org/10.1016/j.labeco.2017.04.007.   [61]

Hurley, M. (2001), "Reviewing Integrated Science and Mathematics: The Search for Evidence and Definitions From New Perspectives", *School Science and Mathematics*, Vol. 101/5, pp. 259-268, https://doi.org/10.1111/j.1949-8594.2001.tb18028.x.   [43]

Jenkins, J. et al. (2019), "Boosting school readiness: Should preschool teachers target skills or the whole child?", *Economics of Education Review*, Vol. 65, pp. 107-125, http://dx.doi.org/10.1016/j.econedurev.2018.05.001. [44]

Jennings, J. and J. Bearak (2014), ""Teaching to the test" in the NCLB era: How test predictability affects our understanding of student performance", *Educational Researcher*, Vol. 43/8, pp. 381-389, http://dx.doi.org/doi.org/10.3102/0013189X14554449. [92]

Kaldi, S., D. Filippatou and C. Govaris (2011), "Project-based learning in primary schools: effects on pupils' learning and attitudes", *Education 3-13*, Vol. 39/1, pp. 35-47, https://doi.org/10.1080/03004270903179538. [47]

Kärkkäinen, K. (2012), Bringing About Curriculum Innovations: Implicit Approaches in the OECD Area, *OECD Education Working Papers*, No. 82, OECD Publishing, Paris, https://doi.org/10.1787/5k95qw8xzl8s-en. [91]

Kärner, A. et al. (2014), *Principal steps toward curricular freedom in Estonia CIDREE yearbook 2013*, SLO, http://www.cidree.org/cidree_yearbook/yearbook-2013/ [5]

Kirst, M., B. Anhalt and R. Marine (1997), "Politics of Science Education Standards", *The Elementary School Journal*, Vol. 97/4, pp. 315-328, http://dx.doi.org/10.1086/461868. [12]

Kokotsaki, D., V. Menzies and A. Wiggins (2016), "Project-based learning: A review of the litertautre", *Improving Schools*, Vol. 19/3, pp. 267-277, https://doi.org/10.1177/1365480216659733. [48]

Kuiper, W. and J. Berkvens (eds.) (2013), *Moving up the line - Schools at the hub of policy development in Ireland*, CIDREE, http://www.cidree.org/wp-content/uploads/2018/07/yb_13_balancing_curriculum_regulation_and_freedom.pdf. [28]

Kuiper, W. and J. Berkvens (eds.) (2013), *Portugal - The mirage of curricular autonomy*, CIDREE, http://hdl.handle.net/10400.3/2461. [86]

Kuiper, W., N. Nieveen and J. Berkvens (2013), *Curriculum regulation and freedom in the Netherland - A puzzling paradox*, SLO/CIDREE, https://dspace.library.uu.nl/handle/1874/289592. [6]

Kyriacou, C. (2011), "Teacher stress: Directions for future research", *Educational Review*, Vol. 53/1, pp. 27-35, http://dx.doi.org/doi.org/10.1080/00131910120033628. [87]

Laird, T. et al. (2008), "The effects of discipline on deep approaches to student learning and college outcomes", *Research in Higher Education*, Vol. 49, pp. 269-294, https://doi.org/10.1007/s11162-008-9088-5. [37]

Lambert, P. (2001), *Curriculum reform in primary schools: Policy steering in and out of schools*, University of Sydney. [110]

Lavy, V. (2015), "Do Differences in Schools' Instruction Time Explain International Achievement Gaps? Evidence from Developed and Developing Countries", *The Economic Journal*, Vol. 125/588, pp. F397-F424, http://dx.doi.org/10.1111/ecoj.12233. [63]

Lawrence, D., N. Loi and B. Gudex (2019), "Understanding the relationship between work intensification and burnout in secondary teachers", *Teachers and Teaching*, Vol. 25/2, pp. 189-199, https://doi.org/10.1080/13540602.2018.1544551. [75]

Lehrer, R. and L. Schauble (2015), "Learning Progressions: The Whole World is NOT a Stage", *Science Education*, Vol. 99/3, pp. 432-437, http://dx.doi.org/10.1002/sce.21168. [51]

MacPhail, A. and J. Halbert (2005), "The implementation of a revised physical education syllabus in Ireland: circumstances, rewards and costs", *European Physical Education Review*, Vol. 11/3, pp. 287-308, http://dx.doi.org/10.1177/1356336x05056769. [103]

Majoni, C. (2017), *Curriculum overload and its impact on teacher effectiveness in primary schools*, Open Access Publishing, http://doi.org/10.5281/zenodo.290597. [2]

Marhefka, J. (2011), "Sleep Deprivation: Consequences for Students", *J Psychosoc Nurs Ment Health Serv.*, Vol. 49(9), pp. 20-25, http://dx.doi.org/10.3928/02793695-20110802-02. [73]

McDonald, A. (2010), "The Prevalence and Effects of Test Anxiety in School Children", *Educational Psychology*, Vol. 21/1, pp. 89-101, https://doi.org/10.1080/01443410020019867. [94]

Ministry of Education (New Zealand) (n.d.), *Develop smart policy and curriculum documents to support educational improvement*, Ministry of Education, https://www.educationcounts.govt.nz/__data/assets/pdf_file/0004/122539/case-32-complete.pdf. [25]

Moreno, J. (2007), "The Dynamics of Curriculum Design and Development: Scenarios for Curriculum Evolution", in *School Knowledge in Comparative and Historical Perspective*, Springer Netherlands, Dordrecht, http://dx.doi.org/10.1007/978-1-4020-5736-6_12. [38]

Morgan, M. and D. Craith (2015), "Workload, stress and resilience of primary teachers: Report of a survey of INTO members", *Irish Teachers' Journal*, Vol. 3/1, pp. 9-20, https://www.into.ie/app/uploads/2019/07/IrishTeachersJournal2015.pdf. [7]

Muijs, R. and R. Reynolds (2017), *Effective Teaching: Evidence and Practice*, Sage. [104]

NCCA (2010), *Curriculum overload in primary schools: An overview of national and international experiences*, https://ncca.ie/media/2052/curriculum_overload_in_primary_schools_an_overview_of_national_and_international_experiences.pdf. [27]

NCCA (2010), *Curriculum overload in primary schools: Experiences and reflections from the learning site*, https://ncca.ie/media/2053/curriculum_overload_in_primary_schools_experiences_and_reflections_from_the_learning_site.pdf. [84]

Ndura, E. (2004), "ESL and Cultural Bias: An Analysis of Elementary Through High School Textbooks in the Western United States of America", *Language, Culture, and Curriculum*, Vol. 17/2, pp. 143-153, https://doi.org/10.1080/07908310408666689. [99]

Oates, T. (2011), "Could do better: using international comparisons to refine the National Curriculum in England", *The Curriculum Journal*, Vol. 22/2, pp. 121-150, http://dx.doi.org/10.1080/09585176.2011.578908. [9]

OECD (2020), *Education at a Glance*, OECD Publishing, https://doi.org/10.1787/69096873-en. [13]

OECD (2020), *PISA for Schools website - Frequently Asked Questions*, https://www.oecd.org/pisa/aboutpisa/pisa-based-test-for-schools-faq.htm (accessed on 1 November 2020). [109]

OECD (2019), *OECD Future of Education 2030. Making physical education dynamic and inclusive for 2030. International curriculum analysis*, https://www.oecd.org/education/2030-project/contact/OECD_FUTURE_OF_EDUCATION_2030_MAKING_PHYSICAL_DYNAMIC_AND_INCLUSIVE_FOR_2030.pdf. [113]

OECD (2019), *OECD Future of Education and Skills 2030 Curriculum analysis: Progress report on the draft international synthesis report.* [40]

OECD (2019), *OECD Future of Education and Skills 2030. Conceptual learning framework. A series of concept notes*, OECD Publishing, Paris, http://www.oecd.org/education/2030-project/teaching-and-learning/learning/learning-compass-2030/OECD_Learning_Compass_2030_Concept_Note_Series.pdf. [14]

OECD (2019), *OECD Future of Education and Skills 2030: OECD Learning Compass 2030*, http://www.oecd.org/education/2030-project/teaching-and-learning/learning/learning-compass-2030/OECD_Learning_Compass_2030_concept_note.pdf. [18]

OECD (2018), *Education at a Glance 2018: OECD Indicators*, OECD Publishing, Paris, https://doi.org/10.1787/eag-2018-en. [112]

OECD (2017), *Education 2030 - Conceptual Learning Framework: Background Papers*, https://www.oecd.org/education/2030-project/contact/Conceptual_learning_framework_Conceptual_papers.pdf. [42]

OECD (2016), *PISA 2015 Results (Volume I): Excellence and Equity in Education*, https://doi.org/10.1787/9789264266490-en. [66]

OECD (2014), *Education at a Glance 2014: OECD Indicators*, OECD Publishing, Paris, https://dx.doi.org/10.1787/eag-2014-en. [64]

OECD (2014), *PISA 2012 Results: What Students Know and Can Do (Volume I, Revised edition, February 2014): Student Performance in Mathematics, Reading and Science*, PISA, OECD Publishing, Paris, https://dx.doi.org/10.1787/9789264208780-en. [41]

OECD (Forthcoming), *An ecosystem approach to curriculum redesign and implementation (title TBC)*, OECD Publishing, Paris. [108]

OECD (Forthcoming), *Curriculum flexibility and autonomy (title TBC)*, OECD Publishing, Paris. [111]

Parker, J., D. Heywood and N. Jolley (2012), "Developing pre-service primary teachers' perceptions of cross-curricularl teaching through reflection on learning", *Teaching and Learning: Theory and Practice*, Vol. 8/6, pp. 693-716, https://doi.org/10.1080/13540602.2012.746504. [45]

Penuel, W. and L. Shepard (2016), "Social Models of Learning and Assessment", in *The Handbook of Cognition and Assessment*, John Wiley & Sons, Inc., Hoboken, NJ, USA, http://dx.doi.org/10.1002/9781118956588.ch7. [52]

Ramírez, M. (2006), "Understanding the low mathematics achievement of Chilean students: A cross-national analysis using TIMSS data", *International Journal of Educational Research*, Vol. 45/3, pp. 102-116, http://dx.doi.org/doi.org/10.1016/j.ijer.2006.11.005. [78]

Ramsden, P. (1993), "Theories of learning and teaching and the practice of excellence in higher education", *Higher Education Research and Development*, Vol. 12/1, pp. 87-97, https://doi.org/10.1080/0729436930120108. [89]

Rawling, E. (2015), "Curriculum change and examination reform for geography 14-19", *Geography*, Vol. 100/3, pp. 164-168. [11]

Rivkin, S. and J. Schiman (2015), "Instruction time, Classroom Quality, and Academic Achievement", *The Economic Journal*, Vol. 125/588, pp. F425-F448, http://dx.doi.org/10.1111/ecoj.12315. [60]

Rutherford, T., J. Long and G. Farkas (2017), "Teacher value for professional development, self-efficacy, and student outcomes within a digital mathematics intervention", *Contemporary Educational Psychology*, Vol. 51, pp. 22-36, http://dx.doi.org/doi.org/10.1016/j.cedpsych.2017.05.005. [19]

Sahlberg, P. (2016), "The Global Educational Reform Movement and Its Impact on Schooling", in *The Handbook of Global Education Policy*, John Wiley & Sons, Ltd, Chichester, UK, http://dx.doi.org/10.1002/9781118468005.ch7. [101]

Schmidt, W. et al. (2011), *Towards Coherence in Science Instruction: A Framework for Science Literacy*, Michigan State University, https://edwp.educ.msu.edu/wp-content/uploads/sites/34/2020/02/PROMSE-Coherent-Science-PRRvol8.pdf. [39]

Schmidt, W. and R. Houang (2012), "Curricular Coherence and the Common Core State Standards for Mathematics", *Educational Researcher*, Vol. 41/8, pp. 294-308, http://dx.doi.org/10.3102/0013189x12464517. [33]

Schmidt, W., R. Houang and L. Cogan (2002), "A coherent curriculum: The case of mathematics", *American Educator*, Vol. 26/2, pp. 10-26. [30]

Schmidt, W., H. Wang and C. McKnight (2005), "Curriculum coherence: an examination of US mathematics and science content standards from an international perspective", *Journal of Curriculum Studies*, Vol. 37/5, pp. 525-559, http://dx.doi.org/10.1080/0022027042000294682. [29]

Schunk, D. and M. DiBenedetto (2016), "Self-efficacy theory in education", *Handbook of Motivation at School*, Vol. 2, pp. 34-54, https://www.routledgehandbooks.com/doi/10.4324/9781315773384.ch3. [56]

Schwartz, M. et al. (2009), "Depth versus breadth: How content coverage in high school science courses relates to later success in college science coursework", *Science Education*, Vol. 93/5, pp. 798-826, http://dx.doi.org/10.1002/sce.20328. [36]

Segool, N. et al. (2013), "Heightened Test Anxiety Among Young Children: Elementary School Students' Anxious Responses to High-Stakes Testing", *Psychology in the Schools*, Vol. 50/5, pp. 489-499, https://doi.org/10.1002/pits.21689. [93]

Shepard, L., W. Penuel and J. Pellegrino (2018), "Using Learning and Motivation Theories to Coherently Link Formative Assessment, Grading Practices, and Large-Scale Assessment", *Educational Measurement: Issues and Practice*, Vol. 37/1, pp. 21-34, http://dx.doi.org/10.1111/emip.12189. [53]

Silova, I., V. Budiene and M. Bray (eds.) (2006), *Lithuania*, Open Society Institute. [70]

Silver, R. et al. (2011), "Curriculum implementation in early primary schooling in Singapore", *CRPP Research Report*, http://hdl.handle.net/10497/4453. [88]

Simon, M. et al. (2010), "A Developing Approach to Studying Students' Learning through Their Mathematical Activity", *Cognition and Instruction*, Vol. 28/1, pp. 70-112, http://dx.doi.org/10.1080/07370000903430566. [50]

Simon, M. and R. Tzur (2004), "Explicating the Role of Mathematical Tasks in Conceptual Learning: An Elaboration of the Hypothetical Learning Trajectory", *Mathematical Thinking and Learning*, Vol. 6/2, pp. 91-104, http://dx.doi.org/10.1207/s15327833mtl0602_2. [49]

Sparks, S. (2020), *In Many Districts, a Child's Academic Trajectory Is Set by 3rd Grade*, http://blogs.edweek.org/edweek/inside-school-research/2020/02/Academic_mobility_low.html. [80]

Stein, K., T. Kintz and A. Miness (2016), "Reflectiveness, Adaptivity, and Support: How Teacher Agency Promotes Student Engagement", *American Journal of Education*, Vol. 123/1, https://doi.org/10.1086/688168. [107]

Torres, A. (2016), "Is this work sustainable? Teacher turnover and perceptions of workload in charter management organizations", *Urban Education*, Vol. 51/8, pp. 891-914, https://doi.org/10.1177/0042085914549367. [74]

UNESCO (2002), *Building the capacities of curriculum specialists for education reform*, UNESCO, Paris, http://www.ibe.unesco.org/fileadmin/user_upload/archive/curriculum/Asia%20Networkpdf/vienrepor.pdf. [34]

van der Embse, N. et al. (2017), "The influence of test-based accountability policies on teacher stress and instructional practices: a moderated mediation model", *Educational Psychology*, Vol. 37/3, pp. 312-331, https://doi.org/10.1080/01443410.2016.1183766. [106]

van Silfhout, G. (2016), *Ruimte en sturing in het onderwijssysteem*, SLO nationaal expertisecentrum leerplanontwikkeling. [102]

Voogt, J., N. Nieveen and S. Klopping (2017), *Curriculum Overload: A Literature Study*, Unpublished OECD Reference Document. [1]

Wang, D. (2014), "The New Curriculum and the Urban-Rural Literacy Gap", *Chinese Education and Society*, Vol. 44/6, pp. 87-101, https://doi.org/10.2753/CED1061-1932440606. [98]

Weiner, B. (1972), "Attribution theory, achievement motivation, and the educational process", *Review of educational research*, Vol. 42(2), pp. 203-215. [59]

Wigfield, A. et al. (1997), "Change in children's competence beliefs and subjective task values across the elementary school years: A 3-year study", *Journal of Educational Psychology*, Vol. 89/3, pp. 451-469, http://dx.doi.org/doi.org/10.1037/0022-0663.89.3.451. [58]

Zarmati, L. (2019), *Future of Education and Skills 2030: Curriculum analysis. Learning progression in history*, https://www.oecd.org/education/2030-project/about/documents/Learning%20progression%20in%20history%20-%20Zarmati.pdf. [81]

Zee, M. and H. Koomen (2016), "Teacher Self-Efficacy and Its Effects on Classroom Processes, Student Academic Adjustment, and Teacher Well-Being: A Synthesis of 40 Years of Research", *Review of Educational Research*, Vol. 86/4, pp. 981-1015, http://dx.doi.org/doi.org/10.3102/0034654315626801. [20]

Zhen, R. et al. (2010), "Trajectory patterns of academic engagement among elementary school students: The implicit theory of intelligence and academic self-efficacy matters", *British Journal of Educational Psychology*, http://dx.doi.org/doi:10.1111/bjep.12320. [57]

How do countries compare?

Countries/jurisdictions experience curriculum overload in a variety of ways depending on their national contexts and circumstances. This section focuses on comparing different country/jurisdiction approaches to accommodate emerging societal needs into the curriculum[1]. It first presents an overview of which cross-curricular themes and competencies are articulated in curricula as well as how countries/jurisdictions make different choices on embedding them in existing learning areas so as to avoid further expanding of the already overcrowded curricula. The section then delves into different country/jurisdiction approaches to structure subject-specific goals in curricula and their potential impact on the content overload as perceived by teachers.

WHAT KINDS OF CROSS-CURRICULAR THEMES DO COUNTRIES/JURISDICTIONS ARTICULATE TO ACCOMMODATE NEW DEMANDS?

Figure 11 provides an overview of the most frequently selected cross-curricular themes across countries/jurisdictions participating in this study.

These themes also reflect the efforts of countries/jurisdictions to refresh their vision of education, echoing the Education 2030 Learning Compass. Some of the most frequent themes, including "**environmental education, sustainability**" and "**local and global citizenship, peace**", reflect efforts to accommodate 21st century challenges in curricula through cross-curricular themes. Cross-curricular themes are also used to promote holistic development of students beyond traditional learning. This is articulated through cross-curricular themes like "**health education, well-being, lifestyle**" or through value-based themes like "**moral/values education**" or "**cultural identity and multiculturalism**".

The granularity of themes included in curricula also varies across countries/jurisdictions. Most countries/jurisdictions include broad themes, such as "**ICT and media**" in Denmark and "**environmental education**" in the Czech Republic. Others complement these with more specific themes, such as "**road/safety education**" in Mexico and "**consumer education**" in Brazil.

There are also differences across countries/jurisdictions in the number of cross-curricular themes that are articulated. British Columbia (Canada), for example, highlights just one cross-curricular theme, that of "Indigenous knowledge and perspectives". Australia articulates three layers of national priorities: "**Aboriginal and Torres Strait Islander histories and cultures**"; "**Asia and Australia's engagement with Asia**"; and "**sustainability**".

Social, cultural and historical contexts are articulated using country-specific themes like: "**Indigenous knowledge and perspectives**" in British Columbia (Canada), "**Cultural identity**" in Estonia, "**Unification education**" in Korea and "**Education on ethnic-racial relations and history and culture of Afro-Brasileira, African and Indigenous peoples**" in Brazil (Table WEB 12[2]).

HOW DO COUNTRIES/JURISDICTIONS EMBED SUCH CROSS-CURRICULAR THEMES INTO EXISTING SUBJECTS?

Countries/jurisdictions vary not only in the type and number of cross-curricular themes that they articulate, but also in how these themes are embedded into existing subjects. The following sections describe how the cross-curricular themes of "**environmental literacy/literacy for sustainable development**", "**physical/health literacy**", "**ICT/digital literacy**", "**computational thinking/programming/coding**", "**career education/work studies**", and "**media studies**" are embedded into curricula across countries and jurisdictions.

Environmental literacy/literacy for sustainable development

Environmental and sustainability education is found to be one of the most articulated cross-curricular themes as part of the general goals of education (Figure 11). Increasing concerns about climate change and local impacts might also explain why certain countries/jurisdictions have introduced new subjects specifically devoted to sustainable education, as in New Zealand.

Figure 11 **Types of cross-curricular themes reported by countries/jurisdictions**

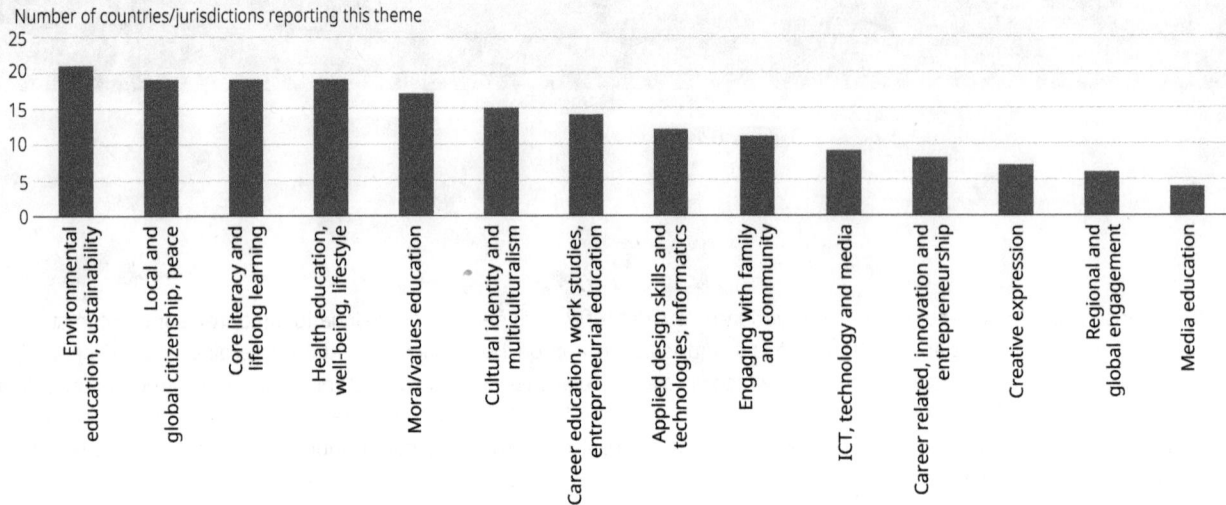

Note: Values displayed include only countries/jurisdictions with responses that could be clearly coded as yes/no. Ordered in descending order of number of countries reporting this theme.
Source: Data from the PQC, item 1.1.2.4.
StatLink https://doi.org/10.1787/888934195815

This focus on sustainable development is echoed in content items within traditional subjects; it is consistently mapped at moderate levels across curricula (Figure 12). Most countries/jurisdictions embed it in more than 20% of the curriculum. China embeds sustainable development in roughly 45% of the mapped curriculum, while Estonia and Japan embed it in nearly 40% of their curriculum.

Sustainable development literacy is found mostly in the areas of humanities, sciences, and technologies/home economics. Israel and Portugal only include sustainable development within the areas of humanities and sciences. Notably, China embeds sustainable development literacy across six out of the seven mapped learning areas.

Physical and health literacy

Nineteen (out of 37 countries) countries/jurisdictions embed health literacy as a cross-curricular theme into existing subjects (Figure 11). In doing so, nearly all countries/jurisdictions, unsurprisingly, predominantly embedded physical/health literacy in the subject of **physical education/health** (e.g. in British Columbia [Canada] and Japan). In Portugal and the Russian Federation, **science** is the subject that carries most of the items related to physical/health literacy. In some countries/jurisdictions including Estonia, Northern Ireland (United Kingdom) and Kazakhstan, physical/health literacy is widely distributed across subjects. (Figure 13)

Hungary and Ireland created a new subject to foster students' ability to maintain and develop their well-being as well as to adopt **a healthy lifestyle**. These subjects might be seen as a potential tool to counterbalance new threats to the health and well-being of the young population, such as increasing stress related to academic performance and risks associated with the widespread use of technologies in social interactions. In other countries, **health education** is not a separate subject but is mainly combined in the curriculum with **physical education**, as in Australia, Chile, Japan, Ontario (Canada), Wales (United Kingdom) and China (OECD, 2019[1]).

Figure 12 **Literacy for sustainable development in curricula**

Distribution of content items in the mapped curricula targeting literacy for sustainable development (as main or sub target), by learning area

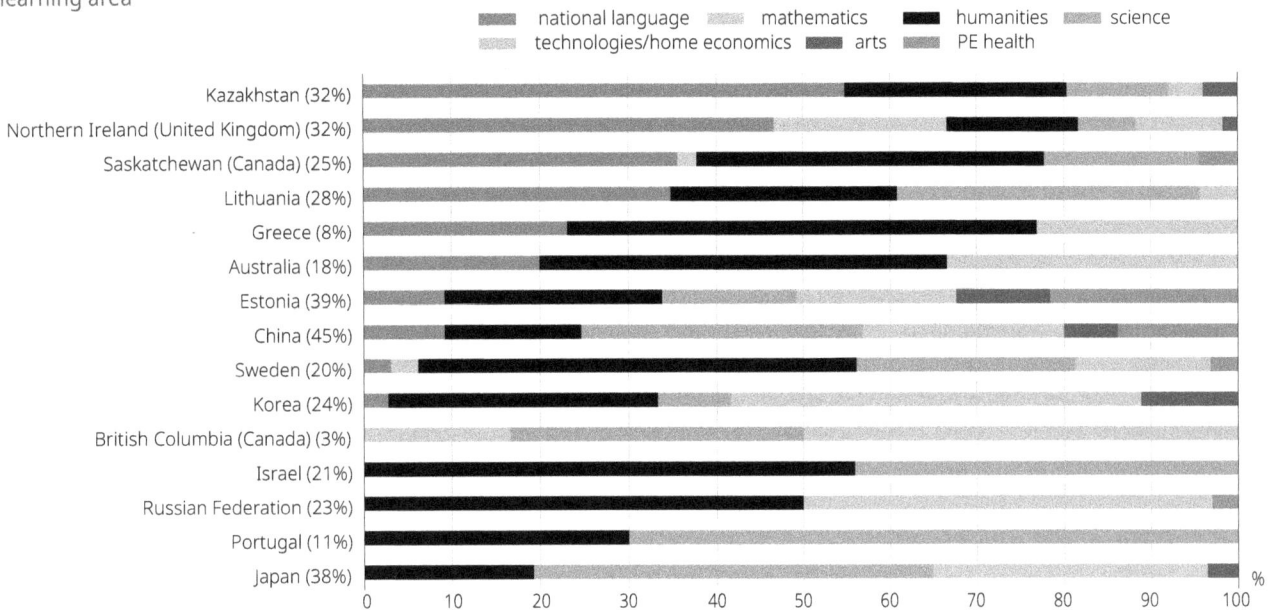

legend: national language, mathematics, humanities, science, technologies/home economics, arts, PE health

Note: The percentage next to the name of the country/jurisdiction refers to the total percentage of the mapped curriculum that embeds the competency. Ordered by decreasing percentage of items mapped in national language.

Source: Data from the Education 2030 Curriculum Content Mapping exercise.

StatLink https://doi.org/10.1787/888934195834

Figure 13 **Physical/health literacy in curricula**

Distribution of content items in the mapped curricula targeting physical/health literacy (as main or sub target), by learning area

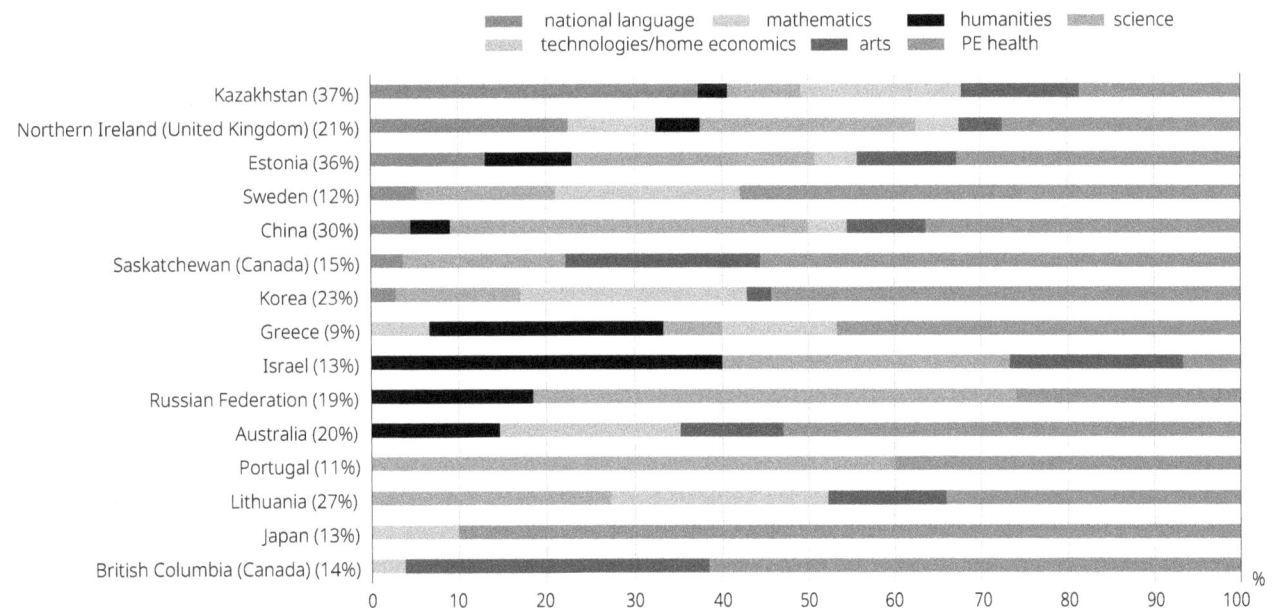

legend: national language, mathematics, humanities, science, technologies/home economics, arts, PE health

Note: The percentage next to the name of the country/jurisdiction refers to the total percentage of the mapped curriculum that embeds the competency. Ordered by decreasing percentage of items mapped in national language.

Source: Data from the Education 2030 Curriculum Content Mapping exercise.

StatLink https://doi.org/10.1787/888934195853

ICT/digital literacy and technologies, informatics

Nine (out of 37) countries/jurisdictions include it as a cross-curricular theme (Figure 11), and some reflect it in subject-specific content items. ICT/digital literacy is strongly emphasised within the content of mapped curricula. In most countries/jurisdictions, over 30% of the curriculum embeds this competency (Figure 14). Estonia stands out because of the stronger emphasis given to ICT/digital literacy in its curriculum (almost 70% of the mapped curriculum items embed it). In Estonia, science and humanities are the two most highlighted learning areas for the development of ICT/digital literacy. In these areas, ICT literacy is not highlighted as a subject-specific education goal. Yet, it is still embedded in around 20% of the items in each. To reinforce ICT literacy, Estonia adopts a three-sided approach, including it as a cross-curricular competence, a cross-curricular theme and a stand-alone subject.

Korea and Kazakhstan also strongly highlight ICT/digital literacy in their mapped curricula (just below 60% of the items include it). In Kazakhstan, mathematics is particularly highlighted as a space to develop ICT/digital literacy (with just above 30% of the items).

A noticeable pattern across participating countries/jurisdictions is, that ICT/digital literacy is consistently embedded in most of the seven mapped learning areas. In general, countries/jurisdictions take many opportunities to foster ICT competency in their curricula. It is frequently embedded in the domains of both science, technology, engineering and mathematics (STEM) and social sciences (such as humanities and national language). The presence of this competency is less prevalent in some of the mapped areas, notably in physical education/health and arts (with a lower percentage of items incorporating it across countries/jurisdictions).

Figure 14 **ICT/digital literacy in curricula**

Distribution of content items in the mapped curricula targeting ICT/digital literacy (as main or sub target), by learning area

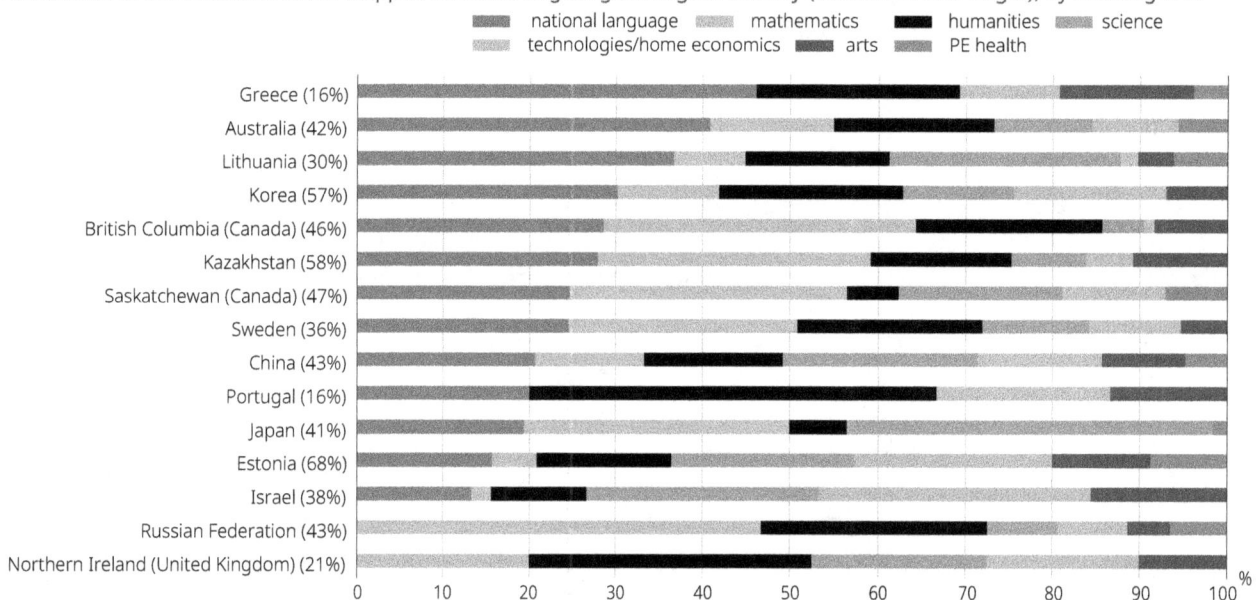

Note: The percentage next to the name of the country/jurisdiction refers to the total percentage of the mapped curriculum that includes the competency. Ordered by decreasing percentage of items mapped in national language.
Source: Data from the Education 2030 Curriculum Content Mapping exercise.
StatLink ⟐📊 https://doi.org/10.1787/888934195872

Computational thinking/programming/coding

With the increasing presence and use of big data, students need not only to be literate in data and technologies but also to be creators, programmers and users of data, consistent with the co-agency model of knowledge creation put forth by the OECD Learning Compass 2030. The European Commission suggests that the demand for workers with specialist digital skills, such as computational thinking, programming and coding is growing by about 4% each year (Berger and Frey, 2015[2]).

Computational thinking/programming/coding is closely linked to ICT/digital literacy. This may explain why only Poland explicitly embeds programming as a cross-curricular competency and theme. In other countries, coding or competency is usually accounted for under broader competencies or themes such as ICT or IT skills.

Figure 15 **Computational thinking/programming/coding in curricula**

Distribution of content items in the mapped curricula targeting literacy for computational thinking/programming/coding (as main or sub target), by learning area

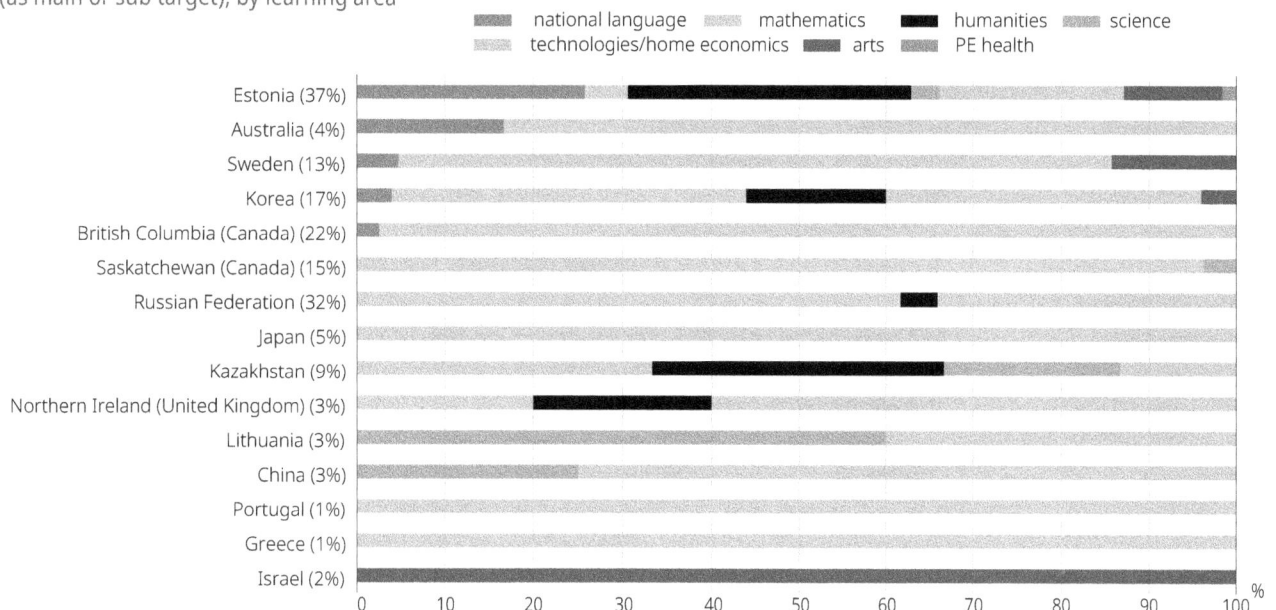

Note: The percentage next to the name of the country/jurisdiction refers to the total percentage of the mapped curriculum that embeds the competency. Ordered by decreasing percentage of items mapped in national language.
Source: Data from the Education 2030 Curriculum Content Mapping exercise.
StatLink https://doi.org/10.1787/888934195891

Coding and computational thinking are not explicitly highlighted as a cross-curricular topic or as a stand-alone subject. While higher than entrepreneurship, computational thinking/programming/coding does not have a large degree of integration into the mapped curriculum (Figure 15).

The majority of countries/jurisdictions have low levels (below 10%) of computational thinking/programming/coding embedded in their curriculum, but the proportion is much higher in Estonia (37%) and the Russian Federation (32%). Estonia has a triple approach for embedding ICT in its curricula, including it as a cross-curricular theme, a competency and a stand-alone subject. This reinforced approach ensures that ICT skills do not get "lost" among other curricular priorities. As a result, even if coding/computational thinking is not explicitly considered a competency or theme, it appears quite frequently across content items in all subjects of the mapped curricula.

Computational thinking/programming/coding is almost exclusively covered in the technology/home economics and mathematics learning areas. However, Israel only includes it in arts, but to a very limited extent.

Career education, work studies, entrepreneurial education

Relative to other cross-curricular topics, entrepreneurship is only modestly embedded within traditional subjects in a large set of countries/jurisdictions. Half of those participating in the CCM include this cross-curricular topic in less than 10% of the content items in their mapped curricula. This includes Greece, Lithuania, Northern Ireland (United Kingdom), Portugal, Saskatchewan (Canada), Sweden and China (Figure 16).

Other countries have put emphasis on entrepreneurship and embed it in a much higher proportion of the content items in their mapped curricula, as in Estonia (40%) and Japan (56%). This cross-curricular focus on entrepreneurship is articulated with a holistic approach. Both countries embed entrepreneurship across most learning areas in their curricula, including national language, humanities, science, technologies/home economics and arts. In Estonia, this approach is combined with a specific subject for entrepreneurship, which also exists in other countries, such as Korea.

In nearly all countries/jurisdictions, entrepreneurship is embedded within technologies/home economics. A substantial number also use humanities as a platform to embed entrepreneurship. Yet, countries/jurisdictions do not appear to take every opportunity within curricula to tackle entrepreneurship. Learning areas such as mathematics or science are rarely used to embed entrepreneurship.

Figure 16 **Entrepreneurship in curricula**

- -

Distribution of content items in the mapped curricula targeting entrepreneurship (as main or sub target), by learning area

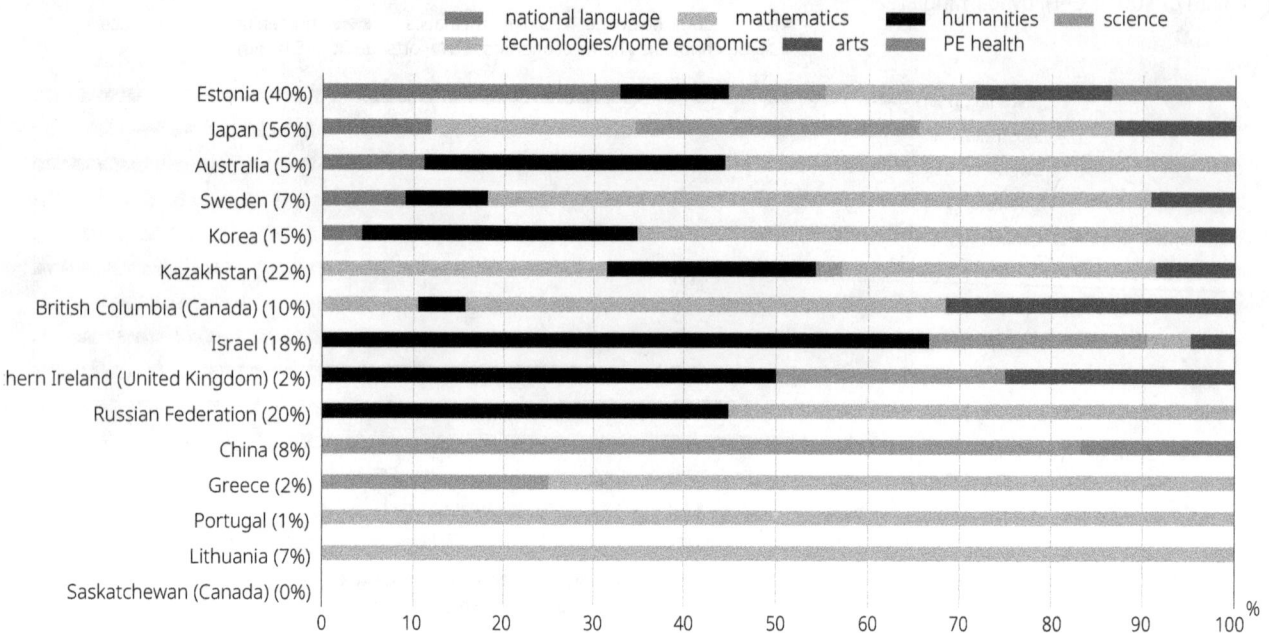

Note: The percentage next to the name of the country/jurisdiction refers to the total percentage of the mapped curriculum that embeds the competency. Ordered by decreasing percentage of items mapped in national language.

Source: Data from the Education 2030 Curriculum Content Mapping exercise.

StatLink https://doi.org/10.1787/888934195910

Figure 17 **Media literacy in curricula**

- -

Distribution of content items in the mapped curricula targeting media literacy (as main or sub target), by learning area

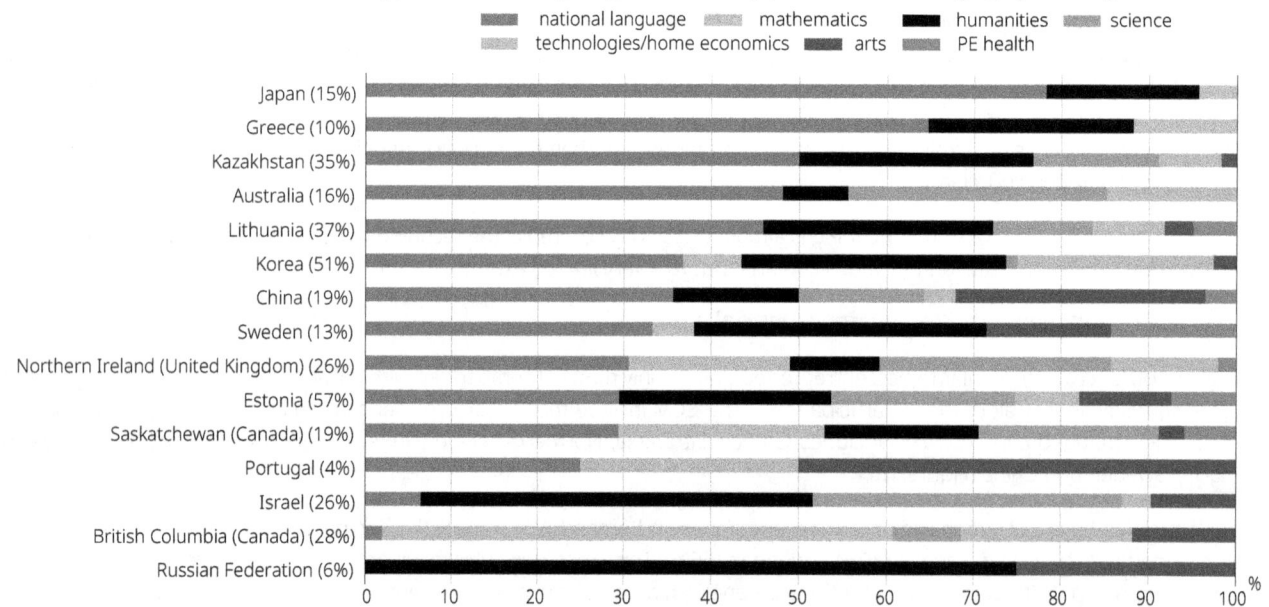

Note: The percentage next to the name of the country/jurisdiction refers to the total percentage of the mapped curriculum that embeds the competency. Ordered by decreasing percentage of items mapped in national language.

Source: Data from the Education 2030 Curriculum Content Mapping exercise.

StatLink https://doi.org/10.1787/888934195929

Media education

There is a growing need to manage the wave of fake news and digital technologies transforming traditional news media. There are growing demands for schools to develop students' media literacy. The competency of media literacy is defined as the ability to derive meaning from and assess the credibility of multiple media sources through critical thinking (OECD, 2019[3]).

In the countries/jurisdictions that participated in the PQC, media education is not frequently explicitly embedded in curricula, as either a cross-curricular topic or stand-alone subjects. The Czech Republic, Denmark, Quebec (Canada) and Northern Ireland (United Kingdom) embed it as a cross-curricular theme. Northern Ireland (United Kingdom) has introduced media education as a stand-alone subject and in Australia, 'Media Arts' is one of five subjects in the Curriculum for The Arts.

However, media education is usually addressed in traditional subjects in the countries/jurisdictions participating in the CCM. In most other countries/jurisdictions, media literacy is present in about 20% to 30% of their mapped curriculum. Two countries, Korea and Estonia, embed it in more than 50% of the mapped curriculum.

Media literacy is mostly embedded in two or three learning areas, such as national language, humanities or technology/home economics (Figure 17). Notable exceptions are two Canadian jurisdictions (British Columbia and Saskatchewan), which include media literacy in mathematics, and the Russian Federation, which includes media literacy only in humanities and arts.

Media education has been introduced as one of the five subjects of the Curriculum for the Arts in Australia, where 16% the mapped curriculum embeds media literacy, and in Northern Ireland (United Kingdom) (26%) (Figure 17).

WHICH CROSS-CURRICULAR COMPETENCIES DO COUNTRIES/JURISDICTIONS MOST COMMONLY SELECT?

In addition to translating societal needs through cross-curricular themes, as described above, countries/jurisdictions can also take an outcomes-based approach, by focusing on cross-curricular competencies. Figure 18 provides an overview of the main types of cross-curricular competencies that countries/jurisdictions articulate in their curricula. Some of the most frequent competencies, including "**social/civic and global competency**", "**co-operation and collaboration**", and "**communication**" reflect efforts to prepare students to successfully navigate an increasingly globalised world. Less common, however, were the competencies of "**information/data literacy**" and "**literacy for sustainable development**" which will be necessary for confronting major societal changes and global challenges.

Figure 18 **Types of cross-curricular competencies reported by countries/jurisdictions**

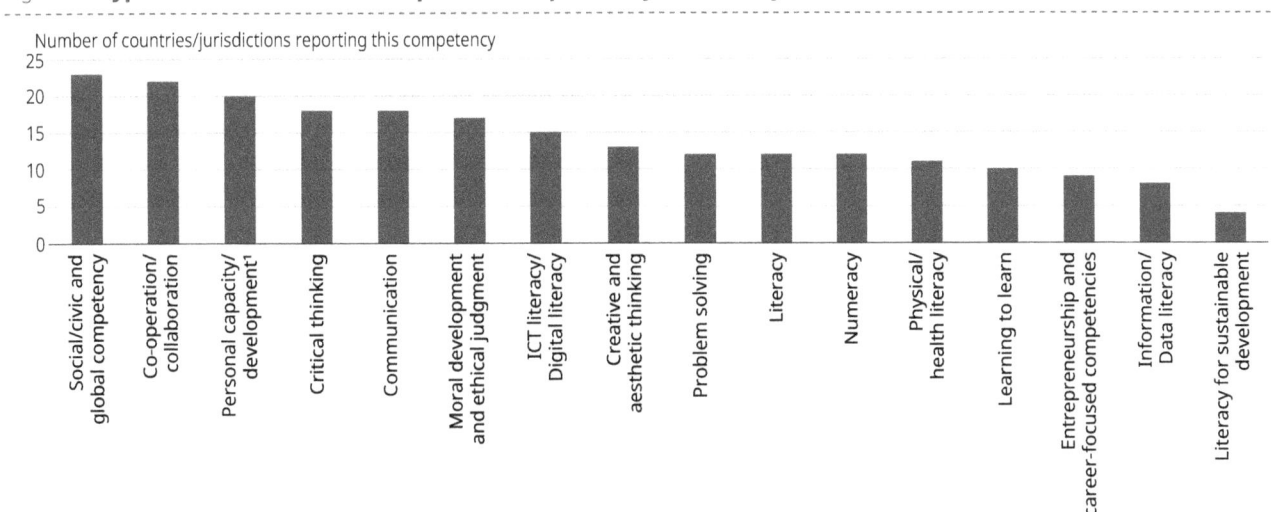

Note: Values displayed include only countries/jurisdictions with responses that could be clearly coded as yes/no. Ordered in descending order of number of countries reporting this competency.

1. Personal capacity/development: i.e. self-regulation/self-control, autonomy

Source: Data from the PQC, item 1.1.2.

StatLink https://doi.org/10.1787/888934195948

Countries/jurisdictions vary with respect to the number of cross-curricular competencies that they articulate and embed in curriculum, ranging from just three in British Columbia (Canada) ("Communication", "Thinking" and "Personal and social competency"), Denmark ("Understanding of citizenship", "Sustainability" and "Understanding of own and others' cultures) and South Africa ("Personal and social well-being", "Physical education" and "Creative arts") to 21 competencies in Sweden (Table WEB 13[3]).

HOW DO COUNTRIES/JURISDICTIONS EMBED CROSS-CURRICULAR COMPETENCIES INTO EXISTING CURRICULUM?

Countries/jurisdictions vary as to the specific ways in which they embed in their curricula the cross-curricular competencies presented in Figure 18 above. The following sections describe how the cross-curricular competencies of "local and global citizenship/peace", "taking responsibility", "co-operation and collaboration", "reconciling tensions and dilemmas", "creating new value", "data literacy", and "financial literacy are embedded into the curricula of the countries/jurisdictions that participated in the curriculum content mapping exercise.

Local and global citizenship, peace

Global competency is defined as the capacity to examine local, global and intercultural issues, to understand and appreciate the perspectives and worldviews of others, to engage in open, appropriate and effective interactions with people from different cultures and to act for collective well-being. In a world increasingly scarred by threats to civilian life and peace, there is an urgent need for students to develop global competencies, including empathy, tolerance and respect for others.

Indeed, promoting peace and sustainable development through education is now enshrined in the **United Nations Sustainable Development Goal Target 4**. Global competency is widely recognised as an important tool for navigating the 21st century, and assessment frameworks such as the **PISA global competence framework** have explored to support the quality, equity and effectiveness of educational systems to create a shared respect for human dignity (OECD, 2019[4]).

The degree to which countries/jurisdictions consistently embed these items in traditional subjects (Figure 19) is typically within 20% to 30% of the curriculum areas and ranges from 8% to 57%.

Figure 19 **Global competency in curricula**

Distribution of content items in the mapped curricula targeting global competency (as main or sub target), by learning area

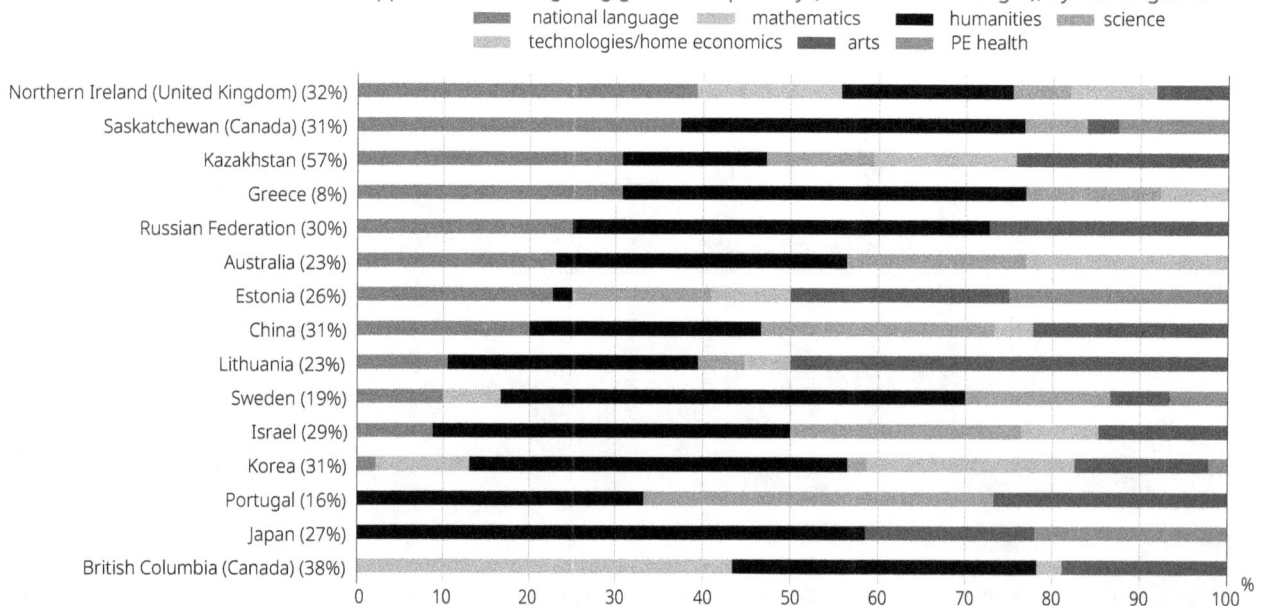

Note: The percentage next to the name of the country/jurisdiction refers to the total percentage of the mapped curriculum that embeds the competency. Ordered by decreasing percentage of items mapped in national language.
Source: Data from the Education 2030 Curriculum Content Mapping exercise.
StatLink https://doi.org/10.1787/888934195967

Global competency is embedded across many of the learning areas, with humanities, national languages, science and the arts being the largest domains. Only Greece (8%), Portugal (16%) and Sweden (19%) have global competency embedded in less than 20% of the mapped curriculum.

Taking responsibility

As globalisation continues and advances in artificial intelligence change the labour market, people will need to rely even more on their capacity for creativity and take responsibility for their own learning throughout their life. Achievement at school also depends on a number of social and emotional skills, such as responsibility. The concept of "taking responsibility" refers to the ability to act responsibly for a good cause, building on principles and integrity for individual and collective well-being.

The degree of representation of responsibility in national curricula varies among countries/jurisdictions with the highest figures in Estonia (68%) and China (54%) and the lowest in Portugal (5%) (Figure 20). Japan, which already covers this concept in a separate study area (Special studies), still includes it in a total of 11% of content across national language, science, technologies/home economics and physical education/health. Students are also often encouraged to take responsibility through extra-curricular activities, such as clubs or volunteering opportunities.

Other areas that countries/jurisdictions have developed include interdisciplinary courses and activities, such as courses in International co-operation, Social entrepreneurship, and Production and development of commodities and services offered in Norway.

Special activities comprise diverse opportunities for students to actively engage in school life through student council and co-operating in activities such as the preparation of lunches or cleaning of classrooms. Portugal proposes opportunities to learn about institutions and democratic participation, and Kazakhstan includes classes on law at ISCED 3 level. What these subjects have in common is that they often foster collaboration and involve students taking on responsibilities. Some also concern the creation of new value by students or building of trust between students and/or in local and national institutions.

Figure 20 **Taking responsibility in curricula**

Distribution of content items in the mapped curricula targeting taking responsibility (as main or sub target), by learning area

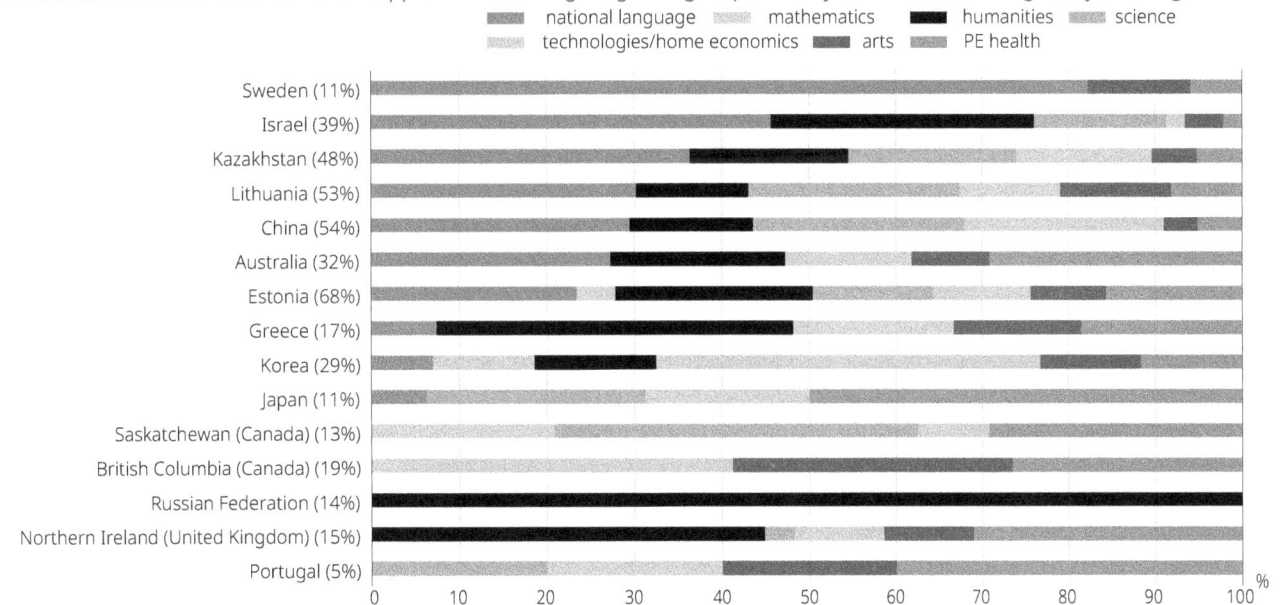

Note: The percentage next to the name of the country/jurisdiction refers to the total percentage of the mapped curriculum that embeds the competency. Ordered by decreasing percentage of items mapped in national language.

Source: Data from the Education 2030 Curriculum Content Mapping exercise.

StatLink https://doi.org/10.1787/888934195986

Co-operation/collaboration

Taking responsibility in a class context is also linked to collaborating successfully with others. Collaboration is a strong predictor of overall student well-being and perceptions of success. Students' abilities to collaborate and work well in a team or a group are often deemed character traits and skills, rather than moral values or attitudes, but they are nonetheless malleable and can be fostered in schools. The OECD Study on Social and Emotional Skills also makes an explicit connection to the importance of collaboration for student success and well-being (Kankaraš and Suarez-Alvarez, 2019[5]).

While high degrees of co-operation/collaboration and teamwork are more common in curricula, particularly in Korea (71%) and Northern Ireland (55%) (Figure 21), other countries, such as Norway, have created specific subjects to reinforce, for example, the theoretical underpinnings of international co-operation.

Across all the participating countries/jurisdictions, collaboration is widely and relatively uniformly embedded across multiple learning areas, with the exception of mathematics. Other ways to support collaboration and teamwork in schools lie in the use of more co-operative pedagogies, such as project-based learning, and the provision of extra-curricular opportunities involving collaboration, such as drama clubs.

Figure 21 **Co-operation/collaboration in curricula**

Distribution of content items in the mapped curricula targeting co-operation/collaboration (as main or sub target), by learning area

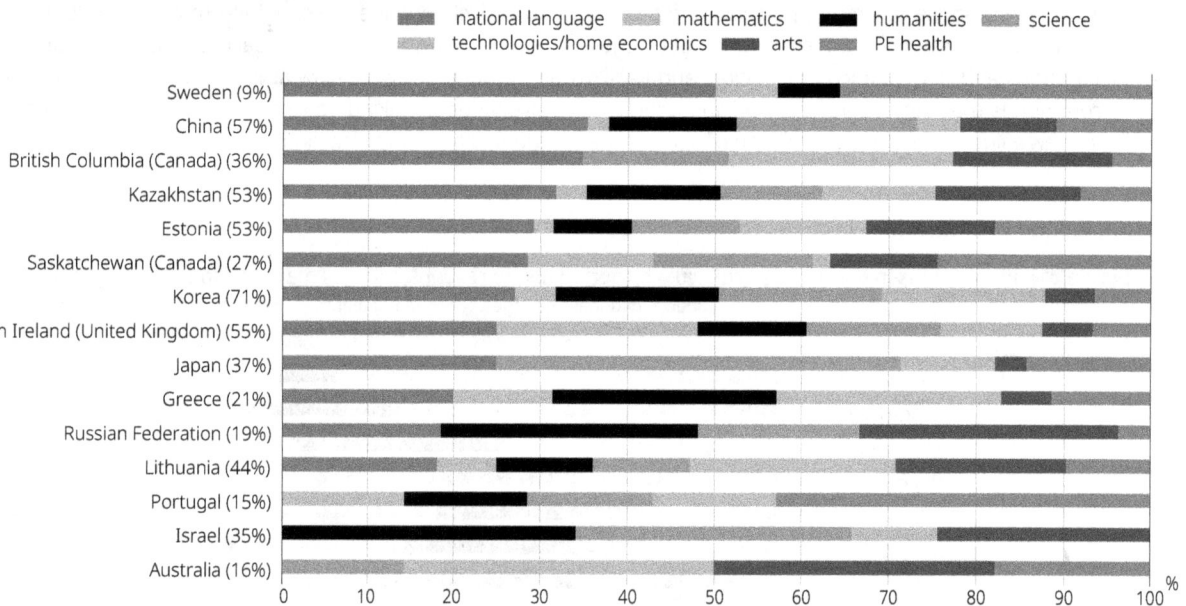

Note: The percentage next to the name of the country/jurisdiction refers to the total percentage of the mapped curriculum that embeds the competency. Ordered by decreasing percentage of items mapped in national language.
Source: Data from the Education 2030 Curriculum Content Mapping exercise.
StatLink ᵐˢᴾ https://doi.org/10.1787/888934196005

Reconciling tensions and dilemmas

Reconciling tensions and dilemmas means taking into account the many interconnections and inter-relations between seemingly contradictory or incompatible ideas, logics and positions, and considering the results of actions from both short-term and long-term perspectives. Through this process, students acquire a deeper understanding of opposing positions, develop arguments to support their own position and find practical solutions to dilemmas and conflicts. Living in a digitalised world requires reconciling tensions, such as the paradox of a world that is increasingly interconnected and the rise of social isolation, or the emergence of a "post-truth" culture in an era of a nearly limitless media sources.

Relative to other transformative competencies, reconciling tensions and dilemmas is given only a modest focus in curricula. It is represented within only 3% to 33% of content items in the mapped curricula of the countries/jurisdictions (Figure 22).

Dilemmas for which students need to consider competing viewpoints are more frequently presented in curricula within humanities and national language. Mathematics and science, learning areas traditionally regarded as exact, are rarely used in curricula as platforms for students to reconcile tensions and dilemmas. One exception is the curriculum of Saskatchewan (Canada), where mathematics is frequently used to foster this transformative competency. In some countries/jurisdictions, such as Portugal, science and humanities are used almost equally to encourage students to reconcile tensions and dilemmas.

Figure 22 **Reconciling tensions and dilemmas in curricula**

Distribution of content items in the mapped curricula targeting reconciling tensions and dilemmas (as main or sub target), by learning area

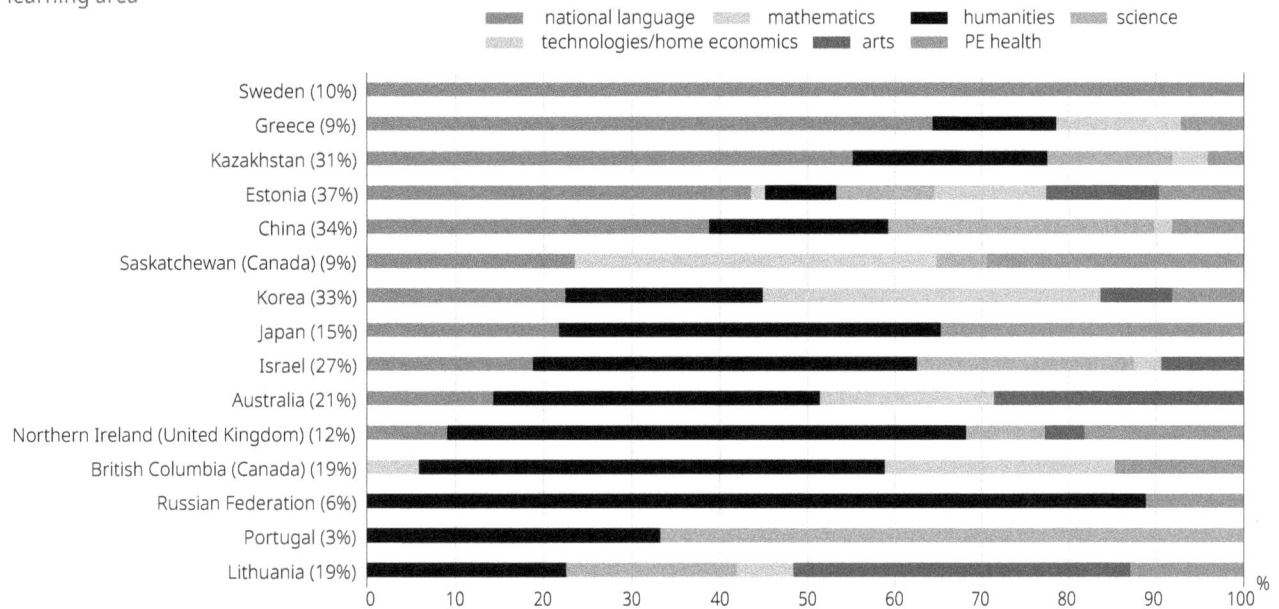

Note: The percentage next to the name of the country/jurisdiction refers to the total percentage of the mapped curriculum that embeds the competency. Ordered by decreasing percentage of items mapped in national language.

Source: Data from the E2030 Curriculum Content Mapping exercise.

StatLink ▤ https://doi.org/10.1787/888934196024

Figure 23 **Creating new value in curricula**

Distribution of content items in the mapped curricula targeting creating new value (as main or sub target), by learning area

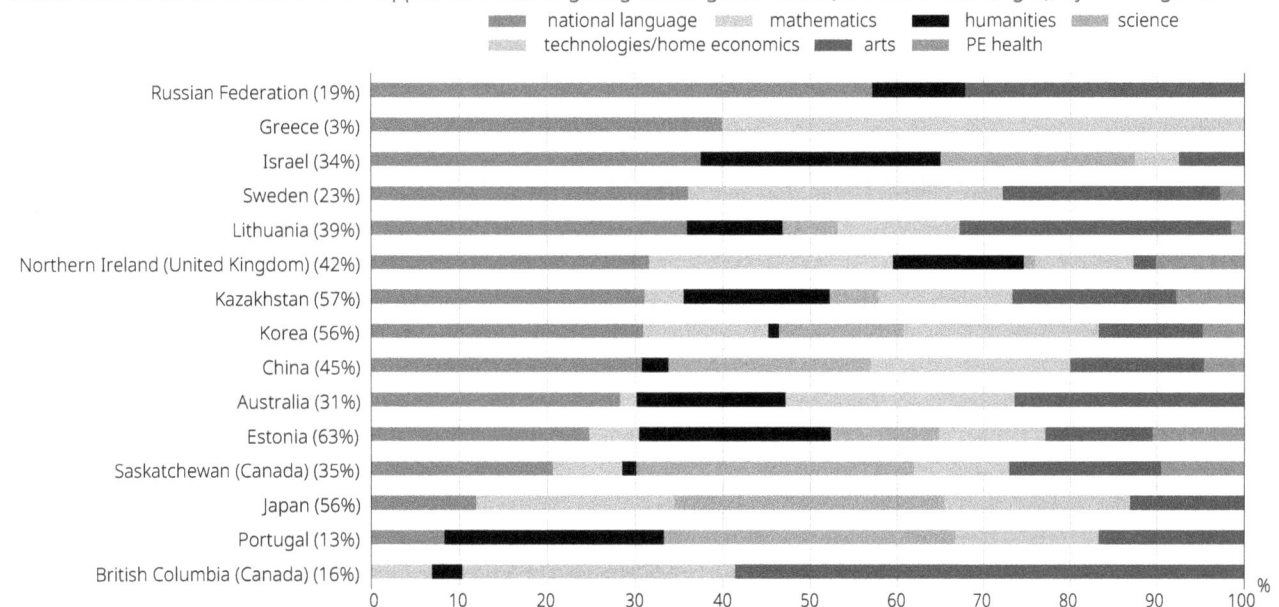

Note: The percentage next to the name of the country/jurisdiction refers to the total percentage of the mapped curriculum that embeds the competency. Ordered by decreasing percentage of items mapped in national language.

Source: Data from the Education 2030 Curriculum Content Mapping exercise.

StatLink ▤ https://doi.org/10.1787/888934196043

Creating new value

The transformative competency of "creating new value" refers to the ability to add value to society by identifying new sources of growth to prepare for 2030, such as developing new solutions, new products and services, new jobs, new processes and methods, new ways of thinking and living, new enterprises, new sectors, new business models and new social models. This competency is necessary in societies that continue to become more diverse and more interdependent, and in economies where the impact of new technologies requires new levels of skills and human understanding. Jobs that require creative intelligence are less likely to be automated in the next couple of decades (Berger and Frey, 2015[2]).

While a majority of countries/jurisdictions recognise the importance of this competency, only some have already acted on it. The degree of mapped curriculum tied to creating new value is typically moderate, ranging from 3% to 63%. Most countries report levels above 30%. Estonia (63%) and Kazakhstan (57%) show the highest occurrence of creating new value across learning areas (Figure 23).

Many countries/jurisdictions embed the competency of creating new value in national languages, technologies/home economics and arts. Norway, for example responds to the need for students to acquire this competency by proposing the subject of "Production and development of commodities and services".

Data literacy

Data literacy is the ability to derive meaningful information from data, to read, work with, analyse and argue with data, and to understand "what data mean, including how to read charts appropriately, draw correct conclusions from data, and recognise when data are being used in misleading or inappropriate ways" (Carlson et al., 2011[6]). Data literacy is a part of the core cognitive foundation of the OECD Learning Compass 2030. Data are being produced at unprecedented rates, and learners need the ability to process, interpret and generate data in order to learn and create.

Information/data literacy is explicitly embedded as a cross-curricular competency in Ireland, Korea, Northern Ireland (United Kingdom), Portugal, Poland, Québec (Canada), Sweden and Singapore. No country/jurisdiction participating in the PQC explicitly embedded this topic as a cross-curricular theme or as a stand-alone subject.

Data literacy is consistently present in content items within mapped curricula of countries/jurisdictions participating in CMM (Figure 24). In most of them, it is embedded in almost 20% of the mapped content items, and in Kazakhstan in as much as 70% of the curriculum, followed by Estonia, the Russian Federation and British Columbia (Canada), all with over 50% of the mapped curriculum embedding this competency.

In Kazakhstan, the two most emphasised learning areas for the development of data literacy are mathematics (26% of the items) and national language (18%). In Estonia, the two most prominent areas for data literacy are national language (26%) and science (27%). In the Russian Federation, a single area, mathematics, carries over 40% of the items that foster data literacy. In British Columbia (Canada), mathematics (29%) and humanities (27%) are the areas that play the biggest role in developing data literacy.

In a subset of countries/jurisdictions, one STEM subject is privileged as the main home for data literacy, carrying at least 40% of the items that embed that competency: mathematics in Saskatchewan (Canada), Portugal and Russian Federation; science in China, Israel and Lithuania; and technology/home economics in Greece.

In contrast, in Japan, the strongest role is given to national language, which carries 62% of the items that embed data literacy. This is reflected in subject-specific education goals. In Japan, information management is frequently highlighted as a specific-subject goal in languages.

Financial literacy

In light of global trends, schools are under mounting pressure to modernise their curricula so that students can develop a broader set of knowledge, skills, values and attitudes to help them cope with new realities and new demands. Particularly following the global financial crisis in 2008, some sectors of society called for schools to develop students' financial literacy, and it is considered a 21st century skill within the PISA assessment framework (OECD, 2017[7]).

Despite the increasing importance of financial literacy, only Ontario (Canada) reported in PCQ to explicitly embed it as a cross-curricular competency in its curriculum (Table WEB 13)[4]. Mexico, Ontario (Canada) and Argentina reported to include it as a cross-curricular theme (Table WEB 12)[5]. Financial education is rarely a stand-alone mandatory subject as the strategy most often followed by countries who explicitly include it in the curriculum is to embed it into existing subjects (OECD, 2019[8]).

Figure 24 **Data literacy in curricula**

Distribution of content items in the mapped curricula targeting data literacy (as main or sub target), by learning area

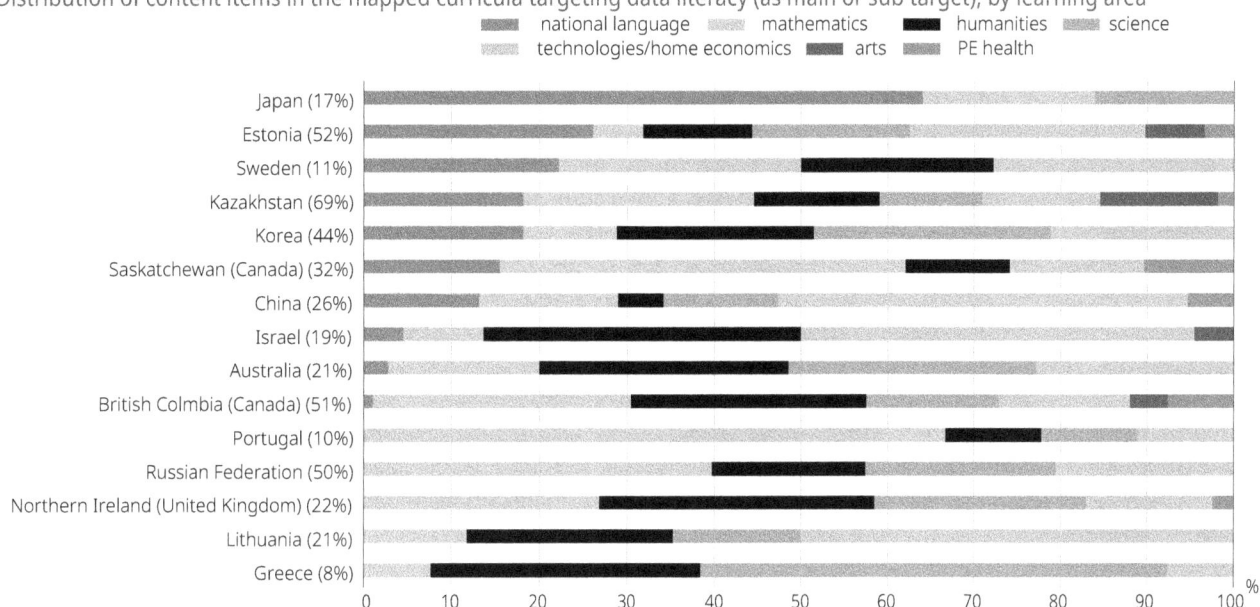

Note: The percentage next to the name of the country/jurisdiction refers to the total percentage of the mapped curriculum that embeds the competency. Ordered by decreasing percentage of items mapped in national language.

Source: Data from the E2030 Curriculum Content Mapping exercise.

StatLink ▨▨ https://doi.org/10.1787/888934196062

Figure 25 **Financial literacy in curricula**

Distribution of content items in the mapped curricula targeting financial literacy (as main or sub target), by learning area

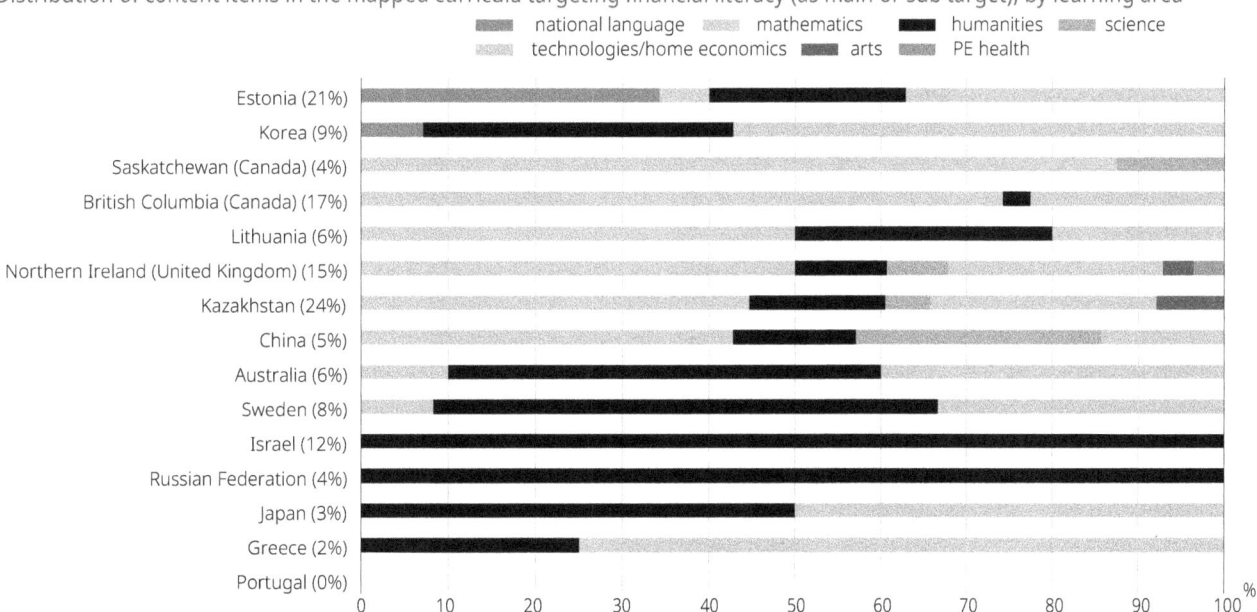

Note: The percentage next to the name of the country/jurisdiction refers to the total percentage of the mapped curriculum that embeds the competency. Ordered by decreasing percentage of items mapped in national language.

Source: Data from the E2030 Curriculum Content Mapping exercise.

StatLink ▨▨ https://doi.org/10.1787/888934196081

> Box 3 **Effects of a new financial literacy programme on student performance**
>
> The effects of exposing students to new literacies are not always clear-cut. In recent years, different OECD countries have included financial literacy programmes in their schools. However, PISA results reveal that there is no correlation between exposure to financial literacy programmes at school and scores on the PISA financial literacy test (OECD, 2014[9]; OECD, 2019[3]).
>
> What are the possible explanations? In the first place, it may be that governments or schools decide to target financial literacy programmes to schools where financial illiteracy is more common, making comparisons difficult (OECD, 2019[3]). Evidence also suggests that students' performance on financial literacy is associated with a wider set of factors, including their family's socio-economic background or societal habits in the communities where they are raised. Indeed, over seven in eight students in every country/economy participating in PISA reported that they receive financial information from their parents, and over two in three students reported that they talk to their parents about their own spending and saving decisions (OECD, 2019[3]).
>
> The weak association between financial literacy performance and financial education may also stem from gaps in curriculum implementation. Most participating countries/economies have enacted national strategies for financial education, but these strategies often give regions, schools and teachers considerable discretion on whether and how to incorporate financial education into lessons. Indeed, financial literacy has emerged only relatively recently as a relevant skill for students and society at large, and it competes for space in already overcrowded school curricula and student timetables with other important skills, such as global citizenship and critical thinking (OECD, 2019[3]). Integrating it successfully will probably require designing curriculum delivery strategies that account for and balance these competing pressures, together with sound evaluation mechanisms to measure the impact of curriculum redesign on students' performance. However, the PISA analysis suggests that creating a specific programme itself may not necessarily be a silver-bullet solution.

Among the mapped in CCM that are motivated by the challenges and demands of the contemporary world, financial literacy is also one of the least targeted in the mapped curricula (Figure 25). Only two countries, Estonia and Kazakhstan, embed it in more than 20% of the mapped curriculum. In most other countries/jurisdictions, financial literacy is present in less than 10% of the mapped curriculum.

In contrast to ICT/digital literacy, emphasis on financial literacy is limited to a narrower set of learning areas in most countries and jurisdictions. Some include it exclusively in one or two learning areas. In Israel and the Russian Federation, it is exclusively embedded in the humanities. In Saskatchewan (Canada), it is mostly embedded in mathematics, with a small percentage of items in science. In Greece and Japan, it is mostly embedded in humanities and technologies/home economics. There is no clear-cut relationship between the exposure of students to a financial literacy programme and the actual student performance (see Box 3), and therefore curriculum designers can be reminded of the general rule 'the more is not the better'.

HOW DO COUNTRIES/JURISDICTIONS STRUCTURE AND DESCRIBE SUBJECT-SPECIFIC GOALS?

Curriculum misalignment can have a substantial impact on curriculum overload. Lack of clarity regarding curriculum changes and their intentions may cause confusion among teachers about the relationship between traditional and newly introduced components of the curriculum. This confusion can force teachers to prioritise one or the other (Voogt, Nieveen and Klopping, 2017[10]).

One example is the 2007 New Zealand Curriculum, in which teachers did not receive guidance on how to connect 21st century competencies with a subject-based curriculum. They thus perceived it as two separate curricular requirements (Sinnema, 2011[11]; Insook and Kang, 2017[12]; Voogt, Nieveen and Klopping, 2017[10]), which led some teachers to prioritise one aspect over the other, thereby undermining the intent of the curriculum.

How countries structure and describe subject-specific goals can result in content overload. If teachers and school leaders fail to understand the demands of the new curriculum and lack the ability to adapt it to their local context in meaningful ways, students may be left with an unmanageable amount of content to be learned. This is likely to lead to a sense of overload, a lack of purpose and overall dissatisfaction with school life. When subject-specific goals are reinforced by grades, stages as well as achievemet levels, and are described too detailed with too much specifications, teachers may feel the pressure to teach materials that will meet all the goals set out in the curriculum. As a result, students may experience content overload. On the contrary, when goals are specified much less but without clear guidelines nor sufficient support for teachers, they may feel pressured to provide their own specifications, in particular, where from which students may also experience content overload.

The majority of countries and jurisdictions organise subject-specific goals by grades, while several others (e.g. Mexico, Scotland [United Kingdom], Sweden, Singapore and Russian Federation) structure subject goals by achievement levels or benchmarks. Several others combine different approaches. In New Zealand, for example, all learning areas have achievement objectives with the exception of science, which are further differentiated into achievement objectives levels. (Table 5).

While the majority of countries/jurisdictions do not link the objectives with the rubrics/achievement levels, several countries do so. New Zealand, Northern Ireland (United Kingdom), Poland, Sweden, Scotland (United Kingdom), and Russian Federation make these links as a general principle, while others do so rather selectively. For example, Norway chooses to do so for a particular level of education (ISCED 2); Portugal chooses this only for focused learning areas (essential learning); China and Viet Nam for certain subjects.

Across countries/jurisdictions the principles and processes used to set subject-specific achievement objectives vary significantly (Table 6), ranging from holistic statements allowing teachers to further refine objectives in their individual contexts (Australia) to very specific assessment criteria (Finland). Ontario (Canada), for example, sets curriculum expectations, that are designed to be specific, attainable, measurable and relevant. They are measureable based on an achievement chart that includes knowledge and understanding, thinking, communication and application. Achievement of student learning is based on the four levels of the achievement chart, which are then equated to either a letter or a percentage grade.

Some countries/jurisdictions only develop achievement objectives for their core content, as in Chile, Norway, Portugal and Québec (Canada). The objectives are commonly linked in one way or another to national/provincial assessments. Chile, Finland, Ireland, Mexico, Norway and Sweden even emphasise this fact.

Table 5 [1/2] **Structure of subject-specific education goals**

Country/ jurisdiction	By grades	By cycles[2]	By rubrics/ achievement levels
Australia	Yes	Yes, by bands of years	No
British Columbia (Canada)	Yes	No	No
Chile	Yes	Yes, ISCED 1: 1-6, ISCED 2: 7-8, ISCED 3: 1-4 of secondary education	No
Czech Republic	(m)	No	(m)
Denmark	(m)	(m)	(m)
Estonia	Yes	Yes, 1-3, 3-6, 7-9	No
Finland	Yes	No	No
Hungary	Yes	Yes, by stages (primary education: 1-4 and 5-8, secondary: 9-12)	No
Ireland	(m)	Yes, by cycles (Junior Cycle, Senior Cycle, etc.)	(m)
Japan	Yes	No	No
Korea	Yes	No	No
Mexico	No	No	Yes, defined by curriculum standards
Netherlands	Yes, 1-8	No	No
New Zealand	No	Yes	Yes
Northern Ireland (United Kingdom)[1]	Yes	Yes, ISCED 0, ISCED 1: 1-3, 2-5, ISCED 2: 3-7, ISCED 3: GCSE: A-G, Advanced: A-E	Yes
Norway	Yes	Yes, 1-2, 3-4, 5-7, 8-10 (ISCED 1 and 2); at ISCED 3, goals are given at all three years	Yes (for ISCED 2)
Ontario (Canada)	Yes	No	No
Poland	Yes	Yes, by stages (primary 1-3, primary 4-8, general secondary 1-4 or technical secondary 1-5, stage I sectoral vocational 1-3, stage II sectoral vocational 1-2)	Yes, expected at the end of a given stage
Portugal	Yes	No	Subjects with essential learning/core competencies: Yes
Québec (Canada)	Yes, accompanied by progression of learning document	No	No
Scotland (United Kingdom)	No	No	Yes, benchmarks
Sweden	No	No	Yes
Turkey	Yes	Yes, 1-4 (primary), 5-8 (middle), 9-12 (high school)	No
United States[1]	(a)	No	(a)
Wales (United Kingdom)	(m)	No	(m)

Note: 1. Responses for these countries/jurisdictions were submitted by independent researchers, not government administrations.

2. Unless specified otherwise, numbers listed in this column refer to grades.

3. Primary 1 – 3 (lower primary); KS 2: Primary 4 – 6 (upper primary); KS3 : Secondary 1 – 3 (junior secondary); KS4: Secondary 4 – 6 (senior secondary).

Source: Data from the PQC, item 1.1.4.2.

Table 5 [2/2] **Structure of subject-specific education goals**

	Country/ jurisdiction	By grades	By cycles[2]	By rubrics/ achievement levels
Partners	**Argentina**	Yes, 1, 2, 3, 4, 5, 6	No	No
	Brazil[1]	(m)	(m)	(m)
	China (People's Republic of)	English and other foreign languages: Yes	No	Yes
	Hong Kong (China)	No	Yes, by Key Stages[3]	Yes, by learning targets
	Costa Rica	Yes	Yes, by educational cycle (preschool, primary school: I cycle: 1-3, II cycle: 4-6, secondary education: III cycle: 7-9, diversified cycle: 10-11-12)	No
	India[1]	(m)	Yes, by stage	No
	Kazakhstan	Yes	Yes, by ISCED level, vertically coherent	No
	Russian Federation	No	Yes, by stage, primary (1-4, secondary 5-9, high school 10-11)	Yes
	Singapore	No	Yes, by key stage (primary, secondary)	Yes
	South Africa	Yes	Yes, by phase	No
	Viet Nam	Yes	Yes, by stage	Yes, depending on subject

Note: 1. Responses for these countries/jurisdictions were submitted by independent researchers, not government administrations.

2. Unless specified otherwise, numbers listed in this column refer to grades.

3. Primary 1 – 3 (lower primary); KS 2: Primary 4 – 6 (upper primary); KS3 : Secondary 1 – 3 (junior secondary); KS4: Secondary 4 – 6 (senior secondary).

Source: Data from the PQC, item 1.1.4.2.

Table 6 [1/2] **Principles and processes for setting subject-specific achievement objectives**

Country/ jurisdiction	Principles and processes for setting objectives
Australia	Describe what students are typically able to understand and do by the end of each year or band of years. Holistic statements that assist teachers to make balanced judgments about the extent and quality of each student's achievement. Aligned to content and validated as part of curriculum development.
British Columbia (Canada)	They are not directly taught or assessed but used to inform the topics chosen. They link back to the goals of the curriculum for each subject area.
Chile	* structured by actionable contents, skills and attitudes * refer to knowledge, skills and attitudes that allow students to advance in their integral development, by understanding their environment and generating the necessary tools to participate actively, responsibly and critically in it * focus on essential aspects of the subjects * accompanied by "assessment indicators" (conceived as observable aspects of learning) to evaluate the performance of the student * each learning objective has several indicators, since there are multiple performances that can demonstrate that a learning has been developed * indicators are a suggestion, so teachers can choose to modify or complement them
Czech Republic	(m)
Denmark	(m)
Estonia	(m)
Finland	Subject-specific achievement objectives are assessment criteria.
Hungary	The framework curricula defines the expected learning outcomes in two-grade cycles. SMART objectives are not given.
Ireland	"Expectations for students" are included in the assessment guidelines that accompany each specification. "Expectations for students" is an umbrella term that links learning outcomes with annotated examples of student work in the subject or short course specification. When teachers, students or parents looking at the online specifications scroll through the learning outcomes, a link will sometimes be available to examples of work associated with a specific learning outcome or with a group of learning outcomes. The examples will include work that is in line with expectations, above expectations or exceptional. The purpose of the examples of student work is to show the extent to which the learning outcomes are being realised in actual cases. Examples of students' work are selected to illustrate expectations and will have been annotated by teachers.
Japan	The achievement objectives are not stipulated clearly, but competencies to be fostered are stipulated in the goals of each subject.
Korea	Korea adopts the grade cluster system, which has been established in order to break from the rigidity of curriculum organisation and implementation and provide flexibility in organising and implementing the curriculum through interactive connection and collaboration between grade levels. The subject-specific education goals in Korea are structured according to the grade clusters. So the subject-specific education goals are same throughout middle school period. The Ministry of Education begins the process of developing evaluation standards according to the new curriculum. A research and development team comprised of subject experts writes the first draft which goes through numerous reviews and a consultation process before being finalised.
Mexico	Curriculum standards are designed to assume the complexity and graduality of learning, define what students will demonstrate at the end of a school term, as referenced to national and international assessments. They are designed using international standards as a reference.
Netherlands	(a)
New Zealand	NZC: All learning areas have achievement objectives (AOs) in eight levels on fold-out charts at the back of the document. NB: Organisation is slightly different in the online version with each set of AOs being included with the learning area statements. TMOA: The achievement objectives successfully identify the skills and knowledge needed to progress learning. The achievement objectives follow the essence statements in each of the learning areas.
Northern Ireland (United Kingdom)[1]	Relate to the development, application and demonstration of cross-curricular and thinking skills and personal capabilities within and across subjects
Norway	At ISCED 2 for core subjects: They describe the quality of competence in a subject and are based on subject-specific competence aims as described in subject curricula. They are designed to function as a support for teachers in the final assessment of their students and to provide a common national framework for assessment work.

Note 1. Responses for these countries/jurisdictions were submitted by independent researchers, not government administrations.

2. In Hong Kong (China), there are curriculum aims/objectives of each of Key Learning Areas/subjects, not limited to "core contents", but these aims and objectives are linked to national assessments for only some of the Key Learning Areas/subjects (English Language, Chinese Language, Mathematics), and at some Key Stages only (i.e. Key Stage 1 – 3). But for Key Stage 4, the curriculum aims/objectives are linked to the national assessment in all subjects. The nature of the national assessments for Key Stage 1 – 3 (mainly for formative assessment for schools' use) is different from that of Key Stage 4 (which includes a university admissions purpose).

Source: Data from the PQC, item 1.1.4.2.

Table 6 [2/2] **Principles and processes for setting subject-specific achievement objectives**

	Country/ jurisdiction	Principles and processes for setting objectives
OECD	**Ontario (Canada)**	The curriculum expectations are designed to be specific, attainable, measurable, relevant. Expectations are measureable based on an achievement chart which includes knowledge and understanding, thinking, communication and application. Achievement of student learning is based on the achievement chart and the four levels which are then equated to either a letter or a percentage grade.
	Poland	(m)
	Portugal	They exist mainly the subjects with essential learning.
	Québec (Canada)	Define essential knowledge students must acquire and be able to use by the end of each academic year/cycle in terms of subject-specific and cross-curricular competencies. They are set out in the progression of learning document accompanying each secondary school subject.
	Scotland (United Kingdom)	(m)
	Sweden	Must be clear and distinctly designed so that they contribute to an equal assessment. Should be concrete and evaluable but not designed in such a way that they micromanage schools and teachers or restrict teachers' educational freedom. The level of ambition of the knowledge requirements must be adapted to what is realistic within the framework of the total teaching time. The knowledge requirements are based on the long-term goals of the subjects and describe observable performances corresponding with the abilities stated in the goals.
	Turkey	Achievements consist of content dimension and skill dimension. While the achievements are structured, attention has been paid to ensuring that they are as clear as possible (to be understood by everyone alike), a precise and clear single judgment (skill), accessibility, age level, observability and measurability. It includes explanations of the products which are expected to be put forward by the suggestions on the methods and techniques that can be used and on the achievements of the products.
	United States[1]	(m)
	Wales (United Kingdom)	(m)
Partner	**Argentina**	(a)
	Brazil[1]	(m)
	China (People's Republic of)	(a)
	Hong Kong (China)[2]	The process of developing the whole-school as well as KLA and subject curriculum aims, broad learning outcomes and assessment objectives rests with the CDC and its sub-committees for the different KLAs, and for the senior secondary level also with the Hong Kong Examinations and Assessment Authority (HKEAA). In the process, feedback is collected from different stakeholders, including education professionals and the general public.
	Costa Rica	Specify 13 skills that students must develop in the educational process according to the educational cycles. They are specified in the Education Policy "Educating for a New Citizenship" (2015).
	India[1]	(m)
	Kazakhstan	Expected outcomes allow learners to define their individual development pathways considering their individual skills. The expected outcomes are classified and systematised by taxonomy levels ("knows", "understands", "applies", "analyses", "synthesises", "evaluates") to ensure the integration of research, cognitive, practical and emotional-aesthetic ways of exploring the world.
	Russian Federation	* Cross-curricular results presuppose that students are familiar with interdisciplinary notions and universal educational actions (regulatory, learning and communicative) and acquire the ability to use them in learning and social practices. Besides, students should be able to plan and carry out their learning process independently as well as to collaborate with teachers and peers. * Curricular results presuppose that students have specific skills to each subject knowledge, are aware of types of activities aimed at gaining new knowledge within the subject and able to use this knowledge in learning and project activities. Learning should contribute to development of academic thinking skills, introduce students to major theories, develop students' ability to use academic terminology.
	Singapore	Subject-specific goals are based on the disciplinary intent, and reviewed every six years to ensure that the goals are relevant, appropriately sized and meet the needs of students.
	South Africa	(m)
	Viet Nam	(m)

Note: 1. Responses for these countries/jurisdictions were submitted by independent researchers, not government administrations.

2. In Hong Kong (China), there are curriculum aims/objectives of each of Key Learning Areas/subjects, not limited to "core contents", but these aims and objectives are linked to national assessments for only some of the Key Learning Areas/subjects (English Language, Chinese Language, Mathematics), and at some Key Stages only (i.e. Key Stage 1 – 3). But for Key Stage 4, the curriculum aims/objectives are linked to the national assessment in all subjects. The nature of the national assessments for Key Stage 1 – 3 (mainly for formative assessment for schools' use) is different from that of Key Stage 4 (which includes a university admissions purpose).

Source: Data from the PQC, item 1.1.4.2.

Notes

1. The section compares available OECD data and data collected through the OECD Future of Education and Skills 2030 Policy Questionnaire on Curriculum Redesign (PQC) and Curriculum Content Mapping (CCM) exercises on all four dimensions of curriculum overload. This international comparative data can be a starting point for policy makers to inform their efforts in curriculum design and redesign.

2. Table WEB 12. Cross-curricular themes reported by countries/jurisdictions, StatLink: https://doi.org/10.1787/888934196100.

3. Table WEB 13. Cross-curricular competencies reported by countries/jurisdictions, StatLink: https://doi.org/10.1787/888934196119.

4. Table WEB 13. Cross-curricular competencies reported by countries/jurisdictions, StatLink: https://doi.org/10.1787/888934196119.

5. Table WEB 12. Cross-curricular themes reported by countries/jurisdictions, StatLink: https://doi.org/10.1787/888934196100.

References

Berger, T. and C. Frey (2015), *Future Shocks and Shifts: Challenges for the Global Workforce and Skills Development*, OECD Publishing, Paris, http://www.oecd.org/education/2030-project/about/documents/Future-Shocks-and-Shifts-Challenges-for-the-Global-Workforce-and-Skills-Development.pdf (accessed on 3 November 2020). [2]

Carlson, J. et al. (2011), "Determining data information literacy needs: A study of students and research faculty", *portal: Libraries and the Academy*, Vol. 11/2, pp. 629-657, http://dx.doi.org/10.1353/pla.2011.0022. [6]

Insook, C. and H. Kang (2017), "Embedding key competencies in schooling using the new approaches of competency-based curriculum in New Zealand", *Secondary Education Research*, Vol. 65/3, pp. 601-631, http://dx.doi.org/10.25152/ser.2017.65.3.601. [12]

Kankaraš, M. and J. Suarez-Alvarez (2019), "Assessment framework of the OECD Study on Social and Emotional Skills", *OECD Education Working Papers*, No. 207, OECD Publishing, Paris, https://dx.doi.org/10.1787/5007adef-en. [5]

OECD (2019), *OECD Future of Education 2030: Making Physical Education Dynamic and Inclusive for 2030. International curriculum analysis*, OECD, Paris, https://www.oecd.org/education/2030-project/contact/OECD_FUTURE_OF_EDUCATION_2030_MAKING_PHYSICAL_DYNAMIC_AND_INCLUSIVE_FOR_2030.pdf. [1]

OECD (2019), *OECD Future of Education and Skills: Concept Note Core Foundations for 2030*, OECD, Paris, https://www.oecd.org/education/2030-project/teaching-and-learning/learning/core-foundations/Core_Foundations_for_2030_concept_note.pdf. [3]

OECD (2019), *PISA 2018 Assessment and Analytical Framework*, PISA, OECD Publishing, Paris, https://dx.doi.org/10.1787/b25efab8-en. [4]

OECD (2019), *Policy Handbook on Financial Education for Young People in the Commonwealth of Independent States*, OECD Publishing, Paris, www.oecd.org/daf/fin/financial-education/financial-education.htm. [8]

OECD (2017), *PISA 2015 Assessment and Analytical Framework: Science, Reading, Mathematic, Financial Literacy and Collaborative Problem Solving*, Revised edition, OECD Publishing, Paris, https://doi.org/10.1787/9789264281820-en. [8]

OECD (2014), *PISA 2012 Results: Students and Money (Volume VI)*, Organisation for Economic Co-operation and Development, Paris, http://www.oecd-ilibrary.org/content/book/9789264208094-en. [9]

Sinnema, C. (2011), *Monitoring and Evaluating Curriculum Implementation: Final Evaluation Report on the Implementation of the New Zealand Curriculum 2008-2009*, Ministry of Education. [11]

Voogt, J., N. Nieveen and S. Klopping (2017), *Curriculum Overload: A Literature Study*, Unpublished OECD Reference Document, https://thehub.swa.govt.nz/assets/documents/42417_Monitoring-Evaluating-web-06042011_0.pdf. [10]

What types of challenges do countries/jurisdictions face in addressing curriculum overload, and what strategies do they use to address these challenges?

This section outlines the challenges faced by countries and jurisdictions attempting to address curriculum overload, and the strategies they have adopted to address them. They relate to curriculum overload in three areas examined in this chapter: **content expansion, content overload,** and **curriculum pitch and workload**.

It is important to note that the strategies listed are not recommendations, but rather opportunities for countries/jurisdictions to learn from one another, in line with the Education 2030 project's peer-learning mission.

CONTENT EXPANSION: OVERVIEW OF CHALLENGES AND STRATEGIES

To compete for curriculum space, various actors may add pressure to have their own area of interest covered in curriculum, and when governments try to accommodate all of these areas, curriculum can become overcrowded. Countries and jurisdictions articulated the challenge of content expansion and outlined the strategies they have adopted to counteract it (Table 7).

Table 7 **Challenges and strategies related to content expansion**

	Challenge/strategy	Countries/jurisdictions reporting the challenge/strategy
Challenges	Content expansion resulting from new demands from society, particularly from interest groups	Czech Republic, Estonia, Hungary, Ireland, Japan, New Zealand, Ontario (Canada), Québec (Canada), Argentina, Brazil[1], Hong Kong (China), Costa Rica, India[1], Singapore, Viet Nam
Strategies	Creating a subject to accommodate various changing social demands	Chile, Finland, Japan, New Zealand, Norway, Portugal, Mexico, Sweden, Hong Kong (China), Kazakhstan
	Selecting key or core cross-curricular competencies and embedding them into existing subjects/learning areas	Australia, Czech Republic, Estonia, Finland, Ireland, Japan, New Zealand, Norway, Ontario (Canada), Québec (Canada), Wales (United Kingdom), Brazil[1], Argentina, Hong Kong (China), Costa Rica

Note: 1. Responses for these countries/jurisdictions were submitted by independent researchers, not government administrations.
Source: Data from the PQC, findings from the research section

Content expansion: Challenges

A contributing factor to curriculum overload is **content expansion resulting from new demands from society, particularly from interest groups** lobbying for the addition for new subjects or topics (see "What does research say?"). New content is often added without revising the existing curriculum, leading to overload. Subject experts may also put pressure on policy makers to ensure that their subject discipline remains in the curriculum and that its content is expanded. These interest groups can perceive the reduction of subject content or its removal as a threat to their job security or policy influence (see "What does research say?").

Content expansion resulting from new demands from society, particularly from interest groups

Lobby groups in many countries and jurisdictions have put pressure on governments to include new concepts in curriculum, including 21st century skills and competency-based education (as in Hungary and Brazil); digital technologies, coding and a stronger focus on STEM (as in New Zealand); citizenship, health education, coding and digital media literacy (as in Ireland); and social issues (as in Argentina). When countries/jurisdictions accommodate these requests or demands without removing existing content, curriculum becomes overloaded.

- In **Hungary**, lobbying by stakeholders led to the emergence of new literacy content and further subjects being introduced to the curriculum. For example, in the course of developing the National Core Curriculum there were regular discussions with several social organisations. As a result of these discussions, it was decided, for example, that knowledge concerning the Jewish and Roma communities, including the Holocaust, should be emphatically presented in the documents regulating the content of education. Another example of lobbying is that organisations have prepared specific framework curriculum for specific knowledge elements, like education for family life, domestic tourism and leisure activities, or even playing chess. While these are positive efforts, the result is a confusing increase in the number of framework curricula. Substantial reduction in content, shifting from knowledge-centric education to education that offers ready-to-use knowledge is one of the main goals of development.

- **Ireland**'s second-level curriculum was broadened in 1996 to include compulsory citizenship and in 2000 to include compulsory health education. Also in 2000, a new religious education subject was adopted by a large number of schools. Consequently, in many schools, students were studying 12 or more subjects for their final examinations. At the same time, there was pressure on schools from employers and universities to introduce to the curriculum aspects such as entrepreneurial education and key digital skills. Curriculum overload was one of the factors leading to reform of the Junior Cycle (lower secondary education) introduced in 2015.

- In **New Zealand**, curriculum expansion was seen in 2018, with the addition of digital technology to the 2007 New Zealand Curriculum and *Te Marautanga o Aotearoa*. This was a curriculum refresh, introducing a new strand to the existing technology/*hangarau* curriculum, which required reframing of the learning-area statement. Formally integrating digital technology into the curriculum is intended to support young people to develop skills, confidence and interest in digital technologies and lead them to opportunities across the information technology sector. Schools have struggled to find space for the new material in timetables. This issue contributed to the delay some schools encountered in implementing the new content. New Zealand is currently working to provide additional support for schools to understand how this content can be built into school curricula. At the same time, teachers and schools have felt the need to respond to a wide variety of stakeholder demands, including tensions associated with being focused on the future and responding to calls for a move back to the basics (which often, but not always, refers to reading, writing and mathematics).

- **Argentina** notes that curriculum overload is due in part to pressure exerted by external stakeholders to include specific content related to the news and/or social issues (e.g. corruption, abortion, poverty).

- In **Brazil**, there is a movement advocating for the development of competencies and new disciplines that prepare students for the future. However, it is difficult to establish system-wide support among educators for competence-based reform, as some are concerned by lobbying from professional groups and unions (e.g. teachers who teach specific disciplines) that push to ensure that certain content continues to be included in the curriculum. Some educators believe that the "competence educational movement" serves solely to meet the demand of the private sector for human capital.

Content expansion: Strategies

One strategy to address the challenge of content expansion due to societal demands is that of **creating a subject specifically to address new social changes**. Addressing a new theme by creating a specific subject often assures that an issue stands out and does not "get lost" among content within existing subjects. The themes selected as stand-alone subjects within the curriculum vary across countries/jurisdictions (see Table 8).

Creating new subjects, however, can add to the burden of students' and teachers' timetables. To avoid this, another popular approach among countries/jursidictions is to **translate societal needs into cross-curricular themes and/or cross-curricular competencies and embed them into existing subjects or learning areas,** rather than creating new ones (see "How do countries compare?"). However, this strategy may require good guidance to schools on how to embed the articulated themes or competencies into the existing subjects.

Creating a subject to accommodate various changing social demands

A number of countries/jurisdictions recognise the risk of content expansion in response to societal demands and have created new, non-traditional or non-academic subjects to accommodate this expansion. Japan, for example, have created a specific subject in which new curricular content can be introduced without overloading multiple other subjects. Leaving space in curriculum in this way allows for evolving changing societal needs to be accommodated in the curriculum without the need for frequent overhaul. In other countries/jursidictions, the new subjects created reflect themes informed by global trends (e.g. environmental education in Chile), or address needs more relevant to their national contexts (e.g. citizenship education in Chile and Portugal, "mother tongue" instruction in Sweden, and basics of law in Kazakhstan). In some countries, such as New Zealand, schools are given the autonomy to address themes that are particularly relevant within a local context. This strategy can avoid adding to teachers' perception of overload or mistrust in frequent curriculum changes, but it requires design capacity on the part of teachers and school leaders to use the space as intended in the curriculum.

Table 8 **Non-traditional or non-academic subjects taught at ISCED 2 and/or ISCED 3 level in countries/jurisdictions participating in the PQC**

Career education, work studies, entrepreneurial education	Health education, well-being, lifestyle	Local and global citizenship, peace	Environmental education	Media education	Applied design skills and technologies, informatics	Others
Australia	Hungary	Australia[2]	Korea	Australia	Australia[3]	Finland
British Columbia (Canada)	Ireland	Northern Ireland (United Kingdom)[1]	Norway	British Columbia (Canada)	British Columbia (Canada)	Japan
Estonia	Norway	Norway	India[1]	Ontario (Canada)	Ontario (Canada)	Norway
Kazakhstan	India[1]	Mexico		Northern Ireland (United Kingdom)[1]	Estonia	Mexico
Korea		India[1]			Kazakhstan	Portugal
Mexico					Norway	Sweden
Norway						Kazakhstan
Ontario (Canada)						New Zealand
Poland						Hong Kong (China)
Québec (Canada)						
Viet Nam						

Note: This table refers to cases in which new competencies/contents are embedded in the curriculum as separate subjects and not as content integrated into existing subjects.

1. Responses for these countries/jurisdictions were submitted by independent researchers, not government administrations.

2. Civics and citizenship is included in ISCED 1 as part of humanities and social sciences and as a separate subject in ISCED 2 and 3.

3. Media arts, design and technologies, and digital technologies are separate subjects in the curriculum for ISCED 1 and 2.

4. Captures countries/jurisdictions where newly created subjects do not fall under any particular or frequently-mentioned domain.

Source: Data from the PQC, item 1.1.3.1.

- In 2019, curriculum for 11th and 12th grades in **Chile** was updated to respond to emerging national and global developments through the creation of new subjects such as "Sciences for Citizenship", "Geography, Territory and Socio-environmental Challenges", "Participating and Argumentation in a Democracy", "Computational thinking and Programming", "Economics" and others.

- **Finland** offers guidance counselling and optional studies for students in ISCED 2 and ISCED 3.

- **Japan**'s National Curriculum Standards (2017) attempt to address the many social issues in education through a concept called curriculum management. The National Curriculum Standards not only support an interdisciplinary approach within relevant subjects, but also secure time in the curriculum for interdisciplinary learning, through a dedicated subject called "Period for Inquiry-Based Cross-Disciplinary Study" that provides students with opportunities to connect contents across subject areas.

- Secondary schools in **New Zealand** are able to develop their own subjects by selecting from a range of assessment standards to make up a course. Many schools include a subject on sustainability studies for students in ISCED 3. This subject addresses the specific issue of sustainability, drawing from different topical domains such as social sciences or environmental education.

- **Norway** recently added specific subjects in its curriculum, including international co-operation, social entrepreneurship, stagecraft and performance, and production and development of commodities and services. These are also offered as elective subjects in the curriculum of more advanced education levels, starting at ISCED 2.

- **Portugal** offers a subject on citizenship and development that builds on a wide range of mandatory themes that are also found in other subjects, including human rights, gender equality, interculturality, sustainable development, environmental education, health, sexuality, media, institutions and democratic participation, financial literacy and consumption education, road safety, entrepreneurship, risk, world of work, security, defence and peace, animal well-being and volunteering.

- In **Mexico**, schools can offer elective subjects that cater to a variety of topics, including sign language, conflict resolution, chess, poetry and creative writing,

- Reflecting the increasing multiculturalism in their country, **Sweden** offers "mother tongue" instruction to students who have a parent/guardian with a first language other than Swedish, alongside national language (Swedish) and religion as separate subjects.

- In **Hong Kong (China)**, liberal studies was introduced as a core subject in the three-year senior secondary curriculum in 2009 as part of the New Academic Structure in senior secondary education. The subject aims to broaden students' knowledge base and enhance their social awareness through the study of a wide range of issues. The modules selected for the curriculum focus on themes of significance to students, society and the world, designed to enable students to make connections across different fields of knowledge and to broaden their horizons. The learning experiences provided will foster students' capacity for lifelong learning, so that they can face the challenges of the future with confidence.

- **Kazakhstan** offers the elective subject of basics of law for students in ISCED 3.

Table 8 provides an overview of the main emerging themes that countries/jurisdictions have included as new subjects in their curricula. These non-traditional or non-academic subjects include such varied areas as media education, local and global citizenship, and career or entrepreneurial studies.

Translating societal needs into cross-curricular competencies and themes and embedding these into existing subjects/ learning areas

As an alternative (or supplementary) approach to creating a new subject to accommodate societal needs, some countries and jursidictions reported selecting key cross-curricular themes or competencies and embedding these into existing subjects/learning areas. Such an approach has been taken by Estonia, Japan, New Zealand, Norway and Wales (United Kingdom), among others. Generally speaking, a 'theme' comprises types of knowledge and understanding, while 'competency' is a more holistic concept that includes knowledge, skills, attitudes and values (although the distinction is not always clear-cut). Several countries/jurisdictions, including Australia and British Columbia (Canada), take the dual approach of embedding cross-curricular competencies and themes into curriculum (see Table 9).

- The **Australian** curriculum is often presented as a three-dimensional model, composed of: 1) learning areas; 2) cross-curricular themes; and 3) cross-curricular competencies (i.e. general capabilities). The model suggests that students learn all three of these dimensions interdependently, and it organises them through an integrated approach, rather than as stand-alone subjects. Australia has intentionally embedded its seven general capabilities within its eight learning areas. General capabilities comprise an integrated and interconnected set of knowledge, skills, behaviours and dispositions that students develop and use in their learning across the curriculum. They are addressed through the learning areas and are identified in content descriptions wherever they are developed or applied. General capabilities are also identified where they offer opportunities to add depth and richness to student learning via optional content elaborations.

- **British Columbia (Canada)** also combines themes and competencies and labels its curriculum as a "concept-based, competency-driven curriculum", highlighting that competency-development cannot happen in isolation. It states that effective competency-development can only happen if concept acquisition is also emphasised as part of key knowledge.

- **Estonia** embeds cross-curricular competencies into subject areas. For example, the study of mathematics is described as developing not only mathematics competencies but all other general competencies. Estonia's syllabus for mathematics explains how the general competencies are taught through mathematics, (e.g. cultural values: mathematics is a science that unifies different cultures, and students can learn about the works of mathematicians from different countries and eras). In Estonia, cross-curricular themes and competencies are used in combination with new stand-alone subjects to emphasise topics of special importance. This approach is used for information and communications technology (ICT), which is addressed with a holistic approach across the curriculum.

- In **Finland**, phenomenon-based learning has gained attention in curriculum design. In this approach, competency-development is articulated through phenomenon- or theme-based lessons. In this way, subjects are not compartmentalised, but rather broken down into phenomenon-based lessons that address a given theme with a holistic perspective, cutting across subject boundaries. This approach fosters students' competencies by encouraging them to understand, use, and construct different models to interpret and explain human behaviour, the environment and related phenomena, using active-learning pedagogies like small-scale research projects or field trips.

- **Japan** organises the curriculum around three competencies: 1) knowledge and skills; 2) abilities to think, make judgments and express oneself; and 3) motivation to learn and humanity. The curriculum aims to develop these competencies not by adding new subjects, but rather by embedding them in existing subjects.

- **New Zealand**'s curriculum describes five "key competencies": thinking; using language, symbol and texts; managing self; relating to others; participating and contributing. The competencies are broad and flexible, and each includes sub-competencies that are determined contextually. Key competencies include skills, but also emphasise how skills relate to knowledge, attitudes, and values, and how skills can be used in interactions with others in various contexts. The details of how the key competencies are integrated into classroom teaching have been left to schools to determine, though additional guidance is given in supporting materials. The use of these competencies has evolved over time, as they have increasingly been integrated into learning areas and woven together to inform more action-oriented learning such inquiry projects.

- In **Norway**, schools facilitate learning in three interdisciplinary themes: health and life skills; democracy and citizenship; and sustainable development. The goals for what pupils should learn in these topics are stated in the competence goals for individual subjects where this is relevant. Students develop competence related to the interdisciplinary topics by working with issues on various subjects. They gain insight into challenges and dilemmas on these topics. The knowledge base for finding solutions to problems can be found in many subjects, and the topics must help pupils to achieve understanding and see connections across subjects.

- In **Ontario (Canada)**, each curriculum subject includes a section called "cross-curricular and integrated learning" which outlines how the subject's content and expected competencies relate to other subjects. The section also provides specific examples of how cross-curriculum learning can be organised. The government has mandated that new subject areas should not be added but rather embedded across the curriculum, allowing for cross-curricular competencies such as financial literacy.

- As part of the 2020 redesign of the curriculum in **Wales (United Kingdom)**, six Areas of Learning and Experience are accompanied by three cross-curriculum competencies: literacy, numeracy and digital competence. Cross-curriculum competencies are intended to develop high levels of competence, by providing frequent opportunities to develop, extend and apply them across the curriculum.

- **Argentina** is moving from disciplinary to interdisciplinary learning, where teachers can integrate content and emerging knowledge from different subject areas and relate their lessons to local and global issues. Learning goals have been developed by the national authority for every cycle and subject area of compulsory education to help teachers focus on the most relevant content.

- In **Hong Kong, (China)**, STEM education has been strengthened as part of the latest ongoing curriculum renewal. Instead of introducing a new STEM curriculum, enhancement was made by introducing integrated learning and teaching of the curriculum content in the three Key Learning Areas (KLAs) of Science Education, Technology Education, and Mathematics Education. As a result, new curriculum content was added by drawing from and integrating relevant curriculum contents from the three KLAs to avoid curriculum expansion and overlapping.

Table 9 illustrates the different approaches countries/jurisdictions use to embed cross-curricular themes and/or cross-curricular competencies in their curriculum. Currently, the majority have moved to a competency-based curriculum, meaning cross- curricular competencies stand out as a tool of choice to accommodate societal needs while managing curriculum overload. Countries like Japan, Poland and Turkey, as well as India, the Russian Federation and Viet Nam, exclusively emphasise this cross-curricular competency-based approach. However, a majority of countries/jurisdictions combine cross-curricular competencies with cross-curricular themes.

CONTENT OVERLOAD: OVERVIEW OF CHALLENGES AND STRATEGIES

As noted earlier, "content overload" is the most frequently reported form of curriculum overload (see "What does research say?"). Table 10 summarises the challenges faced by countries/jurisdictions in redesigning curriculum to avoid content overload and the strategies they use to address these challenges.

Content overload: Challenges

In many countries/jurisdictions, **an excessive number of subjects** or **an excessive amount of content** are the main drivers of overload. There seems to be broad consensus that curricular content needs to be carefully selected, with a relatively small number of topics, to ensure the depth and quality of students' learning. However, several countries and jurisdictions report that their curricula contain too much content to allow in-depth coverage of all topics. Moreover, reducing the number of topics or subjects can create a perception among some sectors that educational standards or quality are being lowered. These perceptions can easily lead to countries/jurisdictions shifting from content reduction to content expansion and then back again, often associated with election cycles.

Another challenge relates to the **duplication of content across subjects or grades**. This often results from a subject-specific approach to curriculum redesign, where subject experts lead the process with limited cross-subject co-ordination. Teachers of different subjects then cover the same competencies or content without building on the knowledge already acquired from other subjects. In addition, if curriculum is broadly defined without specifying at what grade level content should be addressed, it may lead to duplication of content across grade levels. This can be detrimental to students' learning, as time that should be spent on deepening learning or exploring new competencies can be wasted on repeating the same content (see "What does research say?"). However, it is important to make a clear distinction between unnecessary duplication and purposeful reflection on the same content for furthering and deepening students' understanding of key concepts.

Table 9 **Countries/jurisdictions applying theme-based and competency-based approaches**

| Theme-based approach only | Competency-based approach only | | Both approaches | |
Partner	OECD	Partner	OECD	Partner
China	Japan	India[1]	Australia	Argentina
	Poland	Russian Federation	British Columbia (Canada)	Brazil[1]
	Turkey	Viet Nam	Chile	Hong Kong (China)
			Czech Republic	Costa Rica
			Denmark	Kazakhstan
			Estonia	Singapore
			Finland	South Africa
			Hungary	
			Ireland	
			Korea	
			Lithuania	
			Mexico	
			Netherlands	
			New Zealand	
			Northern Ireland (United Kingdom)[1]	
			Norway	
			Ontario (Canada)[2]	
			Portugal	
			Québec (Canada)	
			Scotland (United Kingdom)[2]	
			Sweden[2]	

Notes: 1. Responses for these countries/jurisdictions were submitted by independent researchers, not government administrations.

2. The country provided the same answer to cross-curricular competencies and cross-curricular themes.

Source: Data from the PQC, item 1.1.2.4.

A disconnect in learning progression for students across different education levels is another challenge that many countries and jurisdictions face. Policy makers report concerns about the lack of coherence of curriculum across different levels (see "How do countries compare?"). Curricula of later levels do not always build upon the learning acquired earlier. This is particularly true for the transition from early childhood education to primary education, but it can also be observed in some countries/jurisdictions at the transition from lower secondary to upper secondary. This lack of coherence in content may be due to limited co-ordination between curriculum developers across different education levels. It may also be due to issues of sequencing in curriculum reform, for example when the curriculum of one cycle has been modified, but the proceeding or succeeding cycle has not.

The manner in which curriculum documents are structured and presented, including the language used, may also lead to a feeling of overload for teachers. The **size and volume of curriculum documents** can be overwhelming in some countries and jurisdictions. This is particularly the case when the curriculum is presented as physical, paper-based documents, limiting teachers' capacity to navigate between sections and search for information. Even if the curriculum document itself is short and written in accessible language, teachers and students can still feel overwhelmed if textbooks are not properly written or do not include the right number and types of exercises. It is important to ensure that the size, volume and quality of textbooks does not impede the efforts to reduce content. The prescriptive nature of the curriculum or the level of detail included may also lead to confusion over what is mandatory and what is not.

Some countries/jurisdictions report **difficulties at local or school levels in prioritising or designing curriculum content**. Schools' responsibility over curriculum design and management is increasing across countries/jurisdictions. This approach to curriculum design has proven to be beneficial for ensuring that the curriculum meets the needs of students and of the local community. However, schools and local education authorities may not always be able to exercise their responsibility as curriculum designers. Additionally, the distinction between core curriculum content and optional content may be unclear for some teachers, who then consider the whole as the required curriculum to cover. Countries/jurisdictions reported that if some teachers feel that they need to implement all of the elements covered in the curriculum, this leaves little room for in-depth coverage of some topics or reviewing content that some students may be struggling with. If schools lack the capacity to prioritise curriculum content from the national curriculum, or are not empowered to do so, this can lead to a perception of overload.

Table 10 **Challenges and strategies related to content overload**

	Challenge/strategy	Countries/jurisdictions reporting the challenge/strategy
Challenges	An excessive number of subjects or an excessive amount of content	British Columbia (Canada), Chile, Japan, Korea, Norway, Wales (United Kingdom), Argentina, Brazil[1], Hong Kong (China), India[1], Kazakhstan, Russian Federation, South Africa, Viet Nam
	Duplication of content across subjects or across grades	Australia, Hungary, Korea, New Zealand, Netherlands, Brazil[1], Russian Federation
	Disconnect in learning progression across different levels of education	Australia, Chile, Ireland, Ontario (Canada)
	Size and volume of curriculum documents	British Columbia (Canada), Ontario (Canada), Portugal, Argentina
	Difficulties prioritising or designing curriculum content at local and school levels	Finland, Ireland, New Zealand, Scotland (United Kingdom), United States[1], Argentina
Strategies	Defining the right number of topics	Australia, British Columbia (Canada), Chile, Ireland, Japan, Korea, New Zealand, Poland, Wales (United Kingdom), Argentina, India[1]
	Selecting topics as key concepts in a crowded curriculum	British Columbia (Canada), Norway, Korea, India[1], Singapore,
	Removing content duplication across grades and across different subjects	Australia, Finland, Korea, Ireland
	Deliberately repeating topics across grades, learning cycles and education levels	Estonia, Ireland, New Zealand
	Piloting efforts to address content overload and review its impact on teaching and learning and well-being	Australia, British Columbia (Canada), Czech Republic, Japan, Scotland (United Kingdom), Brazil[1], Singapore
	Making curriculum documents more accessible by involving teachers in the development process	Chile, British Columbia (Canada), Norway
	Defining the core content at the national level and giving autonomy to schools and local government on content adaptations	Czech Republic, Netherlands, Mexico, Poland, Scotland (United Kingdom), Wales (United Kingdom), Hong Kong (China), Kazakhstan
	Developing schools' capacity to design their own content	Ireland, New Zealand, Scotland (United Kingdom), Argentina, Russian Federation, Viet Nam

Note: 1. Responses for these countries/jurisdictions were submitted by independent researchers, not government administrations.
Source: Data from the PQC, findings from the research section.

Excessive number of subjects or excessive amount of content

Recognising that curriculum space is not unlimited, countries/jurisdictions report that an excessive number of subjects is likely to hinder student learning, as in Korea. Even when curricular requirements are reduced and there is a shift from detailed prescribed content to broader objectives, overload can persist as teachers and students struggle with what they perceive as vague goals, as in Norway.

- In **Korea**, research conducted in 2015 concluded that, despite curriculum improvement efforts in the previous 2009 Revised Curriculum, there had been persistent issues, such as a large amount of learning content in the curriculum and textbooks (Kim et al., 2015[1]). In addition, many middle-school teachers identified curriculum overload as one of the crucial challenges that hindered student learning and innovation of instruction (Kim et al., 2014[2]).

- **Norway's** changes under the Knowledge Promotion reforms of 2006 resulted in a considerable reduction in curriculum requirements, with the focus shifting from detailed learning content to broader objectives. However, evaluation of the reform showed that the subject areas still suffered from overload, with many themes and topics and comprehensive yet vague subject-specific goals.

Duplication of content across subjects or across grades

Several countries/jurisdictions reported that a key overload challenge resulting from the curriculum design process is the unintended duplication of content across subjects or grades. Such duplication can result from a staggered design process, as in Australia, or the lack of specific grade objectives, as in New Zealand. Such duplication can have negative impacts on student learning, as reported by Korea.

- In **Australia**, the curriculum was developed in three phases, and, as a consequence, some duplication occurred in across subjects and grades. For example, content related to map reading occurs in both mathematics and humanities in different grades, and content related to the seasons occurs in mathematics, science and humanities in different grades.

- **Korea** cites challenges with the overlap of content across subject areas. This is linked with the need to reduce education content, and presenting similar or identical themes recurrently in each subject curriculum and textbook has been addressed as a factor that decreases the effectiveness of learning.

- The **New Zealand** Curriculum generally does not specify particular topics or content to be explored at specific ages or stages of learning. This means that decisions about the appropriate contexts for learning are made at the classroom or school level and that, without co-ordination between teachers across a child's education, topics may be repeated or not covered at all. New Zealand's National Monitoring Study of Student Achievement suggests that this is a persistent issue in a number of learning areas. The risk that this flexible curriculum may lead to important topics being missed or repeated without meaningful development is a key driver behind plans to introduce additional content on New Zealand's history into the curriculum. This move responds to concerns that learners could complete schooling without having learned about critical events in the development of their country.

Disconnect in learning progression across different levels of education

Students' learning in one education level should build on their learning in previous levels. Countries/jurisdictions may recognise the importance of coherence in students' learning across educational levels, but experience challenges in achieving this, as reported by Ireland.

- **Ireland** notes the importance of maintaining coherence in curriculum development at different levels. For example, the review of the Irish language curriculum at ISCED 2 (Junior Cycle) was completed before the start of the review of the Irish curriculum at the upper end of ISCED 1. This review is now completed. From September 2019, the new Irish Language Curriculum was in place for all students of primary education and lower and upper secondary education. Maintaining rigour and focus between the two levels will be an area of particular concern in the coming years to ensure smooth and coherent transitions between primary and post-primary schools. High-quality whole-school planning and teacher planning need to underpin the school's work in each curriculum area in order to achieve coherence. Ireland has found this to be challenging for schools.

The size and volume of curriculum documents

Policy makers report that the length of curriculum documents may overwhelm teachers, even if the mandatory curriculum content has been reduced, as in Ontario (Canada). Furthermore, it is important to note that the size and volume of curriculum documents can increase when material such as achievement indicators are included, as in British Columbia (Canada).

- In **British Columbia (Canada)**, teachers viewed the previous provincial curriculum as too detailed and prescriptive, particularly in areas where there was a provincial examination to assess content. As a result, teaching in these areas became very focused on covering the content, without the time to engage in deeper or more hands-on learning. The fullness of the previous curriculum was further complicated by achievement indicators. Many teachers viewed these as another required layer of curriculum.

- **Ontario (Canada)** views one of the issues of curriculum overload as related to the physical size of curriculum documents. Teachers see the size and volume of the documents and perceive that content has been added, when in fact the content has been reduced and there is more support within the document. A deeper understanding of the structure and content of the curriculum may help to clarify that there are more supports built into the curriculum to support teaching and learning.

Difficulty prioritising or designing curriculum content at local and school levels

Insufficient training and limited understanding of national guidelines on how to design an effective, coherent curriculum may both contribute to overload, as reported by New Zealand and Argentina. For example, a school may attempt to cover more context than actually required by the national curriculum. Schools and local authorities may lack the capacity to make informed decisions on what to include in the curriculum or how to prioritise content, as in Finland and Ireland.

- In **Finland**, there was a lot of criticism of the National Core Curriculum for Basic Education 2004 because of curriculum overload, but overload is actually observed to be heavier in local curricula. Professionals preparing curricula at the local level want to add new, up-to-date aspects, but sometimes do not remove any of the previous goals or content.

- **Ireland's** National Council of Curriculum and Assessment (2010) identified the number and nature of curriculum space demands driven at the local level as a crowding factor that can lead to content-heavy teaching and learning.

- The **New Zealand** Curriculum for Grades 1 to 10 is organised in eight learning areas. Short statements set out in broad terms what the learning area is about, the purpose of studying that area and how it is structured. While the learning areas are presented as distinct, this does not limit the ways in which schools structure the learning experiences offered to students. Schools are expected to make use of the natural connections that exist between learning areas and to link learning areas to the values and key competencies. This has led to significant variability in the way curriculum is delivered in schools, and some schools are struggling to develop effective local curriculum with limited guidance from the national curriculum, including how to define the priority contents.

- In **Argentina**, principals and teachers struggle with what to emphasise and what to discard when planning learning opportunities at the school level. Teachers particularly face difficulties in deciding what to teach and how to prioritise. Moreover, in the presence of an expanded curriculum, principals do not have the knowledge and tools to act as curriculum managers at the school level. Principals in Argentina currently do not receive specific training to perform a management and leadership role.

Content overload: Strategies

Countries/jurisdictions have reported a wide variety of strategies to address content overload, including taking proactive efforts to **define the right number of topics** in curriculum. Such an approach can involve rethinking the number and combination of subjects in order to ensure conceptual coherence and limit the risk of content duplication. Recent developments include combining subjects in areas in response to growing social demands from the labour market, rather than conceptual underpinnings, such as STEM (science, technology, engineering, and mathematics). The OECD Education 2030 Working Group on Mathematic Curriculum Analysis suggests that teachers in these disciplines need to have conceptual understanding of each other's discipline (i.e. how students can follow the coherent conceptual sequencing both within and across these subjects). Furthermore, some countries/jurisdictions experience a pushback against approaches driven by labour market needs. A new movement has emerged to integrate arts (liberal arts, language arts, social studies, physical arts, and fine arts and music) into STEM by adding an "A" (for Arts) to the acronym, converting it from STEM to STEAM (OECD, 2020). This initiative aims to broaden the focus of the range of skills students develop prior to entering the workforce.

A growing number of countries/jurisdictions (see "What does research say?") are taking the approach of **selecting topics as key concepts in a crowded curriculum**. These are broad overarching themes that relate to a number of subjects. Key concepts or "big ideas" help ensure overall coherence in the curriculum and thus create criteria for what content should be included and what should be omitted.

To address the challenge of content duplication, some countries/jurisdictions have set up processes to **remove duplicated content across grades and subjects**. This can involve, for example, establishing national committees of subject experts or research teams to identify duplication and decide where curriculum content should be retained and where it should be removed.

While unintended duplication of content was reported as a challenge by some countries/jurisdictions, a number of them take the approach of **deliberately repeating topics across grades, learning cycles and education levels** to reinforce students' understanding of ideas or concepts they are learning. Students learn effectively when curriculum recognises their prior knowledge, skills, and learning progressions. This recognition is reflected in a "spiral curriculum", which allows curriculum space for students to progress through their learning by stages rather than in a rigid, linear progression through each grade. This approach allows for more coherence of curriculum content across grades and thus reduces the risk of unnecessary duplication. It also gives teachers and schools some flexibility to readjust the content to their students' learning progression, so that teachers review content in a meaningful way to deepen students' learning. Such an approach guards against shallow learning over a broad range of topics that results from curriculum overload.

As curriculum overload has become a central issue of curriculum redesign in many countries/jurisdictions, some policy makers are taking the careful approach of **piloting efforts to address content overload and evaluating their impact on teaching, learning and well-being**. Such an approach means that decisions regarding measures to address overload can be informed by evidence on the potential impact on students of these measures.

To address the challenge of lengthy detailed curricular documents that lead to feelings of overload, some countries/jurisdictions focus on **making curriculum documents more accessible by involving teachers in the development process**. Such an approach, which can involve making language clearer or reducing the size of curriculum documents, is designed to make it less onerous for teachers to engage with curriculum.

In some countries/jurisdictions, strategies to address content overload include **defining the core content at the national level and giving autonomy to schools and local government to make adaptations**. Such an approach is designed to raise awareness among teachers and school leaders about what is core content and what is discretionary content and to provide schools with a level of flexibility on curriculum.

Finally, countries/jurisdictions are increasingly making efforts to **develop schools' capacity to design their own content**. Granting schools the autonomy to design curricular content – and supporting them to develop their capacity to do so – means that curriculum content can be less prescriptive, which can, in turn, alleviate content overload.

Defining the right number of topics

In their attempts to reduce overload, Australia, New Zealand and Wales (United Kingdom) now group subjects by learning areas. These groupings help to articulate cross-subject goals or competencies and to promote collaboration and alignment across subjects. They may also help to alleviate assessment overload, as reported by Australia. Grouping subjects in this way, however, requires careful consideration of conceptual coherence, as reported by British Columbia (Canada).

- The **Australian** Foundation-Year 10 curriculum is organised around eight "learning areas", seven "general capabilities" and three "cross-curriculum priorities". Learning areas are groupings of subjects that share common learning goals and achievement standards. Some learning areas, such as English and mathematics, include only one subject, while others include several subjects. For instance, the "Humanities and Social Sciences" learning area includes the subjects of history, geography, economics and business, and civics and citizenship. Moreover, in Australia, where each learning area comprises multiple subjects, an optional achievement standard has been developed for the learning area to reduce the need to report against each subject in the primary years of schooling. An example is found in the Australian Curriculum area "The Arts", which consists of five subjects.

- The curriculum reform implemented in **British Columbia (Canada)** in 2016 shifted the focus of the curriculum from facts and topics to concepts and deeper learning (see "What does research say?"). With this shift, some key subject matter became more or less prominent, and some was shifted and realigned. While some concepts were moved from one grade level to another, in general, most of the development teams considered the existing sequence to be reasonably strong. However, some concepts were moved and combined in different ways to bring better balance to the whole curriculum. This most often happened by raising the conceptual level of the subject matter. For example, the previous British Columbia (Canada) curriculum had a focused physical education area of learning and combined health and career education into a different area of learning. During this most recent revision process, career education was instead turned into a focused area of learning, and a new physical and health education programme was created to take a comprehensive approach towards overall health and well-being.

- In **Japan**, a subject called "Modern and Contemporary History" was created by the revised National Curriculum Standard in high schools in 2018, and it is compulsory for all students in upper secondary schools. The main feature of this subject is that students learn how to understand history by focusing on major changes in history. Previously, students in Japan studied Japanese history in lower secondary schools and world history as a compulsory subject in upper secondary schools. However, with rapidly advancing globalisation, students need to develop the skills to grasp the world and domestic affairs from a wider and mutual perspective and to study modern history related to the origin of contemporary social issues. That is why this new subject was created. This subject combines Japanese history and world history, but with a different approach. If the courses on Japanese history and world history had simply been combined, it would have led to curriculum overload. Instead, the content of this subject has been limited to modern history after the 18th century, when the industrial revolution occurred. This is a good example of how to avoid curriculum overload by focusing on the content of the subject. In addition to this subject, students in upper secondary schools can choose world history or Japanese history to learn history from ancient times, according to their interest.

- As part of the 2020 redesign of the curriculum in **Wales (United Kingdom),** subjects have been replaced by six Areas of Learning and Experience (AoLEs): expressive arts; health and well-being; humanities; languages, literacy and communication; mathematics and numeracy; and science and technology. The AoLEs are not intended to be seen as compartments, but rather as a means of organising the direction for pupils' learning. AoLEs can be included in the scope of other AoLEs and have clear connections between them. Each AoLE should have both a Welsh dimension and an international perspective. By removing distinctions between core and foundation elements of the curriculum, this approach aims to help ensure breadth and encourage appropriate decisions about balance in a child's or young person's learning experience.

Selecting topics as key concepts in a crowded curriculum

Some countries/jurisdictions are centring their curriculum around key concepts or "big ideas" in order to reduce curricular content and alleviate the burden of content overload on teachers and students. For example, British Columbia (Canada) has used the idea of "big ideas" and reduced the number of learning standards in its curriculum. This helps teachers focus on core content and gives them flexibility to add new content, based on their students' needs. Norway identified "core elements" and reduced the number of competence aims in curriculum, while Korea also carefully selected "core concepts" and reduced the content of curriculum to 80% of what it was previously.

- **British Columbia (Canada)** has significantly reduced both the number and specificity of learning standards across the curriculum. In the past, teachers complained about increasing demands for content coverage and lack of flexibility in the curriculum. The 2016 provincial curriculum presents "big ideas" and has fewer topics listed, with less specificity than previous curricula to allow teachers to customise their teaching to their local contexts and students' interests. These "big ideas" represent what students are expected to understand at the completion of their grade and what will contribute to future understanding. Each course has a set of big ideas that provide an umbrella for the content and curricular competency learning standards. For example, one of the big ideas in Grade 8 mathematics is: "Number represents, describes, and compares the quantities of ratios, rates, and percents". One of the big ideas in Grade 9 social studies is: "Emerging ideas and ideologies profoundly influence societies and events". The curriculum is structured around a number of big ideas for each grade, which are applied across the curriculum subjects. Big ideas are designed to generalise key concepts into broader knowledge and know-how (See Figure 4).

- As part of its curriculum renewal process, **Norway** has identified the core elements in subjects as a direct strategy to address curriculum overload and to facilitate in-depth learning. The core elements found in the curricula for each subject describe the most central content and competencies. The number of competence aims has been reduced. The curricula focus more on explorative learning in order to enhance in-depth learning.

- For its 2015 revised curriculum, **Korea** structured and selected the educational content of each curriculum based on appropriateness and rigour. In particular, core concepts for each curriculum and essential academic components were carefully selected and used as a standard to reduce academic content to 80% in proportion to the time allocated for each subject. The associations and links between subjects and domains were presented to promote integrated and comprehensive learning.

- **Singapore** launched the "Teach Less, Learn More" (TLLM) initiative in 2005, which aimed to reduce content in the curriculum to free up time for teachers to use innovative learning techniques and make learning more engaging, effective and motivating for students. As part of a remodelled national education strategy, the initiative promoted individual learning experiences for students rather than rote learning. TLLM was not simply an attempt to reduce content. Rather, it provided top-down support for ground-up initiatives by teachers and schools. For example, it provided schools with the ability to hire more support staff so that teachers could better focus on tailoring lessons to meet the needs of their diverse classrooms. TLLM also reviewed and streamlined syllabuses while retaining appropriate preparation for higher education. It also diversified the curriculum, giving students more choice in subjects and more opportunities to explore their interests. Singapore reviews curriculum content regularly through a syllabus review cycle. These reviews include consulting stakeholders to ensure that the curriculum load is appropriately sized and that support structures for syllabus implementation are adequate. As part of the 1997 "Thinking Schools, Learning Nation" (TSLN) vision, Singapore made reductions to national curriculum content to create instructional time and space for students to learn through inquiry approaches in teaching and learning and place greater emphasis on the development of 21st century competencies.

Removing content duplication across grades and across different subjects

Some countries/jurisdictions, such as Australia and Korea, have set up processes to review curriculum content to identify and remove duplicated content in an effort to reduce curriculum overload. This can involve identifying and removing generic content, as in Australia. The process may involve bringing together subject experts, as in Korea.

- In **Australia**, following concerns raised by some stakeholders as part of a review of the curriculum initiated by the federal government, action was taken to revise the curriculum through a number of strategies, including removing duplication of generic content across the curriculum and amalgamating aspects of some subject areas into broader learning-area constructs. For example, in the primary years of the Australian Curriculum, Humanities and Social Sciences, the individual subjects of history, geography, civics and citizenship and economics and business were amalgamated to form one learning area. This resulted in the refinement and reduction of content such as the development of cross-disciplinary skills.

- **Korea** created a national curriculum guideline research team and a national curriculum framework committee as part of its 2015 curriculum revision. The teams were established to examine and adjust content across subject areas, and subject researchers examined the content and adjusted for potential repetition. A research team for subject curriculum adjustment and a national committee for subject curriculum adjustment were established to examine and adjust content across subject areas. Again, subject researchers examined the content and adjusted for potential repetition.

Deliberately repeating topics across grades, learning cycles and education levels

A growing number of countries/jurisdictions, such as Estonia, Finland, Ireland and New Zealand, have started to recognise the importance of teaching a topic in a way that means students can gradually assimilate it, and they take this into account when developing their curriculum frameworks. For example, some countries/jurisdictions have adopted a gyre or spiral approach to curriculum content redesign whereby topics are not designed to be covered in a discrete way in a particular grade, but are intentionally revisited across grades, learning cycles and education levels to ensure a deepening of students' understanding over time.

- In **Estonia**, the national curriculum design is based on the idea of a gyre or spiral. This means that the content of the new curriculum provides opportunities to review and repeat the most basic knowledge on a topic throughout the curriculum, but each time on the next level of learners' development. This is why the new curriculum is designed by study levels, rather than by classes/degrees. This concept might lead to in-depth learning and mastery of basic skills, which are crucial for learning on the next, higher level of thinking. The national curriculum presents learning objectives and learning outcomes at study stages (Stage I is Grades 1-3, Stage II is Grades 4-6 and Stage III is Grades 7-9). Each school drafts its own curriculum, basing it on the national curriculum. The study stages allow for differentiation and taking into account students' progress and development. At the local level, the school curriculum and subject syllabuses are developed by classes, taking into account differences in classes and students' characteristics.

- **Ireland** uses the spiral curriculum approach, with students returning to the same topic year after year, studied in more depth each year, for example, in social, personal and health education at different levels of schooling.

- The **New Zealand** Curriculum specifies eight learning areas: English, the arts; health and physical education; learning languages; mathematics and statistics; science, social sciences; and technology. Each area has levelled achievement objectives that set out selected learning processes, knowledge and skills relative to the eight levels of learning. These eight levels are not designed by individual grade levels; they are spread out across the 13 years of schooling in New Zealand. This is to accommodate the fact that student progression is not always steady or linear. There is no clear expectation for students to achieve a particular level of knowledge, understanding, and skills by a particular school year. This flexibility is intended to represent progress towards broader outcomes that ultimately amounts to deeper learning. An unintended consequence of this is that teachers can struggle to understand the learning experiences and outcomes that are appropriate for learners.

Piloting efforts to address content overload and evaluating their impact on teaching, learning and well-being

Policy makers in some countries/jurisdictions are taking the careful approach of testing and reviewing the impact of changes to curriculum content on students' learning and well-being. For example, some countries/jurisdictions, such as Brazil, pilot new curriculum content before scaling up. Other countries/jurisdictions, such as Australia, review the impact of curriculum reforms mid-way through the curriculum cycle so that adjustments can be made if needed. Piloting played an important role in Singapore's "Teach Less, Learn More" initiative.

- The first national curriculum in **Australia** was developed in phases from 2008 until 2016, with a mid-cycle review in 2014 prior to its completion. Once the entire curriculum was published, a process for a holistic review cycle was put in place to ensure coherent refinement across the curriculum for primary and lower secondary education. The curriculum refinement process ensures consideration of alignment with a national Early Years of Learning Framework.

- In **British Columbia (Canada)**, as part of the revision process for content topics and skills, development teams are asked to review topics from grade to grade within their area of learning and across multiple subject areas. Curriculum staff bring research and trends to the table to inform this work.

- In the **Czech Republic**, the Ministry of Education is undertaking a complex revision of its Framework Education Program for Basic Education (FEP BEs) from 2016-20, including the piloting of revised versions of FEP BEs in a small group of schools. The Ministry used piloting for previous curriculum reforms (1991-2001, 2000-2004 and 2007). From 2005 to 2006, it conducted an evaluation of the FEP BE and the school education programmes to ensure that they had enough information to use to design the new curricula.

- **Japan** set up a network of research and development schools to foster curriculum innovation and improve the National Curriculum Standards. These schools set their own research themes relevant to developing innovative curricula. They get approvals from the Ministry of Education, Culture, Sports, Science and Technology (MEXT) to carry out empirical experiments on curriculum and implement innovations that are not aligned with the National Curriculum Standards. The research and development schools can introduce a new subject that is not currently included in the National Curriculum Standards. Over a couple of years, they test the feasibility of the subject's content, teaching materials, teaching time, pedagogy, assessments, etc. For example, based on the practices at these schools, MEXT introduced English education in 2008 to all primary schools as part of the revised National Curriculum Standards. This curriculum change was piloted before 2008 in the research and development schools. They examined the curriculum of English education from various perspectives, including whether it would overload the curriculum.

- **Brazil** highlights the value of small-scale development of projects in some schools that serve as role models and pilots to explore practices such as interdisciplinary projects implemented at the initiative of teachers and principals, or by private institutions and systems that prioritise the development of competencies.

- **Singapore** included evidence collection in its "Teach less, learn more" initiative, allowing a pilot batch of 28 schools in 2006 to explore innovative ways of imparting knowledge and skills with a streamlined curriculum. The Research Activist Attachment Scheme was also a hallmark of the initiative. It allowed teachers to acquire know-how in curriculum design and research to give their ideas more rigour and depth. After this phase, the Ignite! phase included 327 schools that began their own school-based curriculum innovations in 2011.

Making curriculum documents more accessible by involving teachers in the development process

As discussed earlier in this chapter, teachers' feelings of overload can result from the sheer volume of curriculum documents to review and digest. Lack of clarity in subject-specific goals, as well as the types of language used to describe the curriculum content, can also contribute to teachers being overwhelmed or misunderstanding the curriculum guidelines. To address these issues, countries/jurisdictions such as Norway are carefully reviewing the text of curriculum documents to clarify meaning and reduce size.

- **Norway** has paid careful attention to content and clear language in revising the curriculum. Teachers have been involved in the process of revising curricula in order to make priorities clearer and to reduce the content. Teachers have also been involved in making the language in the curricula clearer to enable better understanding and a common interpretation.

Defining core content at the national level and giving autonomy to schools and local government to make content adaptations

Some countries/jurisdictions, such as the Czech Republic, Poland, and Wales (United Kingdom), define national minimum requirements or core learning to be covered and offer schools the possibility of adding additional content, should they wish to. Giving schools flexibility on curriculum design helps reduce overload by allowing schools to customise the curriculum to the specific needs of their students and by reducing the pressure of covering the full breadth of the national curriculum.

- The **Czech Republic** has used an approach where the curriculum is essentially at two levels. Obligatory requirements are specified at the national level and then interpreted into school-based curricula at the local level, enabling teachers to meet the requirements based on local needs and circumstances. At the national level, the Framework Education Programme for Basic Education (FEP BE) specifies the concrete objectives, form, length, and basic curricular content of education, as well as general conditions for their implementation. At the school level, school education programmes (SEPs) provide the framework for implementing education in individual schools. Each school head devises a SEP in accordance with the FEP BE that is adapted to the school's individual context.

- In **Poland**, the core curriculum defines the minimum scope of teaching content. The actual scope of teaching content is indicated by the teacher. The task of the subject teacher is to specify the teaching content of the core curriculum, with the prerequisite that the teacher will adapt the scope and method of teaching to the students' abilities. In the Polish education system, teachers are guaranteed autonomy in creation of the curriculum.

- In **Wales (United Kingdom)**, a key strategy employed in the 2020 curriculum reform is to provide guidance rather than specification, to enable greater flexibility for teachers and schools. The content of the curriculum's six Areas of Learning and Experiences and the related Progression Reference Points are not specified in legislation. Instead, the Curriculum for Wales guidance (2020) sets out: 1) the proposed curriculum requirements set out in legislation for all learners to ensure that all schools cover some core learning; 2) guidelines for schools in developing their curricula across all areas of learning and experience; and 3) expectations around assessment arrangements to support learner progression. The intention is that this will allow greater flexibility in adapting the curriculum over time and, in light of evidence about its implementation, making it more sustainable. The new curriculum will be used throughout Wales from 2022.

- In **Hong Kong (China)**, the curriculum recommended by the Curriculum Development Council (CDC) is open and flexible for school-based adaptation to suit a wide range of school contexts. The Education Bureau also provides continuous professional development programmes all year round for teachers, in order to build their capacities in curriculum planning, learning, teaching, and assessment of their subjects. Such professional development programmes serve to ensure that teachers are kept up-to-date on the latest curriculum developments and learning and teaching strategies on the CDC curriculum for their own school-based adoption/adaptation.

Developing schools' capacity to design their own content

In-school capacity for curriculum design is of critical importance to managing curriculum overload. In Ireland, the school self-evaluation process is used to promote evidence-driven curriculum design and implementation at the school level, as well as to cultivate a culture of collaboration and reflective review. New Zealand, Scotland (United Kingdom), and Viet Nam encourage collaboration among schools and peers to develop local capacity for curriculum design. Argentina focuses on professional development of school leaders, including curriculum management.

- **Ireland** introduced school self-evaluation (SSE) in 2011 and made it mandatory from 2012, providing an effective tool to assist schools to engage in a collaborative, reflective process of internal school review. The process requires schools to gather evidence about teaching and learning practices, analyse the evidence and set targets in curriculum areas. SSE enables in-depth analyses of curriculum implementation in schools. It is promoted and supported by the Department of Education and Skills Inspectorate and by the Professional Development Service for Teachers.

- Following the introduction of the 2007 Curriculum, **New Zealand** has focused on supporting schools to develop their curriculum design capability. This has involved encouraging schools to develop cycles of inquiry and improvement, as well as supporting collaboration between schools and between schools and communities.

- In **Scotland (United Kingdom)**, Education Scotland's Chief Inspector published a Statement for Practitioners (2016) which provides clear advice on how teachers should approach planning for learning and assessment, avoiding overly bureaucratic approaches. Local authorities and empowered head teachers are to provide strong leadership at the local level to ensure that curriculum development and delivery are manageable for teachers (Education Scotland, 2016[3]).

- **Argentina** designed a one-year course specifically to train principals on issues related to school management, leadership, curriculum, innovation and related themes. Provinces and schools adapt and contextualise curriculum to their realities, needs and circumstances. Contextualisation is intended to help identify key issues that are relevant for that particular community, reducing curriculum overload without disregarding common learning goals that need to be achieved by all students.

- **Viet Nam** reports that it is working to increase the autonomy of teachers in rearranging curriculum content and structure to better meet the needs of learners, reduce the requirement to memorise data and learn content, and innovate on examinations and assessments to enhance requirements for application of knowledge.

CURRICULUM PITCH AND WORKLOAD: OVERVIEW OF CHALLENGES AND STRATEGIES

A curriculum that is not pitched correctly will have negative impacts on students, as well as workload implications for both students and teachers. A number of countries/jurisdictions reported challenges related to this issue as well as strategies employed to address them (Table 11).

Table 11 **Challenges and strategies related to curriculum pitch and workload**

	Challenge/strategy	Countries/jurisdictions reporting the challenge/strategy
Challenges	Trade-offs between aiming higher and focusing on essentials	Japan, Hong Kong (China)
	Mismatch between the instruction time allocated to a given subject and the amount of curriculum content to be covered	Norway, Québec (Canada)
	Homework overload	Chile, Poland, Kazakhstan
	Teacher overburden as a threat to teacher well-being	Scotland (United Kingdom)
Strategies	Regulating the learning time at school or home	Czech Republic, Finland, Kazakhstan
	Using digitalisation to address teacher overload	Australia

Source: Data from the PQC, findings from the research section.

Curriculum pitch and workload: Challenges

Countries/jurisdictions can struggle to find the right pitch for curriculum. A curriculum without high aspirations or challenging content may cause disengagement among higher-achieving students. But a curriculum with overly ambitious aspirations and a high level of content may cause disengagement among low-performing students, who then risk falling further behind. A number of countries/jurisdictions face challenges relating to **trade-offs between aiming higher and focusing on essentials.** International competiveness and performance on international assessments can lead countries/jurisdictions to set overly ambitious curricular goals or have unrealistic expectations (see "What does research say?").

A **mismatch between the instruction time allocated to a subject and the amount of curriculum content** to be covered can have a negative impact on students' learning and well-being. Teachers in some countries/jurisdictions feel that they do not have time to cover key topics in depth and, in their attempt to touch on all content, they may not have the time to adapt their teaching to students' learning needs. This content-driven approach to teaching can lead to many students progressing through the education system without acquiring the necessary knowledge and skills (see "What does research say?").

Teachers may also feel the need to compensate for limited instruction time by assigning more homework, which can lead to **homework overload**. While some homework may have benefits for students' learning attitudes and motivation (Bempchat, 2004[4]), excessive assignment of homework interferes with students' lives outside of school, including time with friends or family, time for extra-curricular activities and time to rest and sleep. This, in turn, can have a negative impact on students' mental and physical health and overall life satisfaction (Marhefka, 2011[5]).

In addition to these negative impacts on student learning and well-being, increasing curricular demands and content overload also result in a heavy workload for teachers (see "How do countries compare?"). Countries and jurisdictions thus face the challenge of **overburden as a threat to teacher well-being** (see "What does research say?")

Trade-offs between aiming higher and focusing on essentials

Given that the curricula for some countries/jurisdictions are written to cater for the whole ability spectrum of students, they can find it challenging to persuade schools and parents not to aim over-ambitiously for some students. Aiming to teach the whole curriculum to all students in the spectrum may be overly ambitious, and may disadvantage low-performing students, as reported by Hong Kong (China). Reducing curriculum content, on the other hand, can be perceived by stakeholders as lowering educational standards, as was the case in Japan.

- In **Japan**, the Ministry of Education (MEXT) reduced the content of the curriculum in 1998, following a trend towards curriculum reduction since 1977. This was in response to increasing worries among students and parents about curriculum overload, intensified competition for university entrance and growing numbers of students being left behind. The reform decreased both curriculum content and instruction time by selecting and decreasing the content of subjects to create more time to enhance the quality of learning. However, it did not implement sufficient measures to achieve this important objective. The information was not widely publicised, and there were not enough hours of instruction per subject to reinforce the related knowledge and skills. This 1998 curriculum reform was criticised by various stakeholders, including experts, parents and media, and led citizens to be concerned about a decline in academic standards. This criticism was fuelled by Japan's performance in PISA 2003 , which critics felt was unsatisfactory. As a result, the 2008 reform of national curriculum standards led to an expansion of curriculum content compared to the 1998 reform. The issue of curriculum overload has since become intertwined with debates about educational standards and performance, making it an ever more politically sensitive issue. To allow more time for students to repeat lessons, conduct observations and experiments and write reports, Japan's 2008 curriculum reform increased both content related to knowledge and skills and instruction time. The 2017 reform, to be implemented in elementary schools starting in 2020, will further expand the curriculum to cover content related to foreign languages and computer programming and will further increase instruction time.

- Some parents in **Hong Kong (China)** strongly believe that academic success is of paramount importance and should be the prime consideration in education, rather than letting their children follow their own interests and abilities. This exerts a lot of pressure on children. While the senior secondary curriculum is designed to cater to the full spectrum of students' interests and abilities, some schools and parents may not be used to such an idea and still encourage all students to study all content. For weaker students, studying all of the curriculum content may be too onerous.

Mismatch between formal instruction time and the amount of content

In several countries/jurisdictions, including Norway, policy makers report that, given insufficient instruction time, some teachers feel compelled to cover the breadth of the curriculum without ensuring that students have actually acquired the targeted learning goals. In some cases, policy makers' capacity to modify instruction time may also be constrained by policies, regulations or collective bargaining, as in Québec (Canada).

- An evaluation of the 2006 curriculum reform in **Norway** revealed that subjects had a content overload of detailed themes and topics. However, subject-specific aims are still vague. The 2015 Ludvigsen Report, School of the Future, found that the 2006 reform was broad in content, making deep learning challenging. As part of the new curriculum of 2020 (LK20), Norway is looking to enable in-depth learning through a focus on core elements in subject areas. Teachers have complained that it is difficult to get through the curriculum within designated times. This has meant that there has often been insufficient time for students to focus long enough on each topic to acquire good understanding. This is one of the key matters being addressed through Norway's current curriculum reform process.

- In **Québec (Canada)**, teaching time is set out in collective agreements for teachers that are negotiated at the provincial level. Thus, new subjects or new content have to be added within the teaching time set out in the agreements. When the curriculum was reformed in 2001, new subjects or content had to be integrated within the set teaching time, and it was difficult to add new content to a timetable that was already full. With the intention of focusing learning on core topics, more teaching was allocated to French, mathematics and history. This led to some other courses being dropped or regrouped (e.g. biology, ecology and introduction to technology and physics were grouped under "Science and Technology"), and few elective courses were offered.

Homework overload

Poland and Kazakhstan are among a number of countries/jurisdictions reporting that they face a challenge of homework overload. In some countries/jurisdictions, including Chile, teachers are unable to cover the entire curriculum within the school year (despite covering limited depth and using homework to compensate), and students move to the next grade without the necessary learning prerequisites to build upon. This in turn overloads the content of teaching and learning for the following grades.

- In **Chile**, the Ministry of Education conducted curriculum coverage studies in 2011 and 2013 to see how much of the curriculum content of five subjects is actually implemented by schools. These studies showed that none of the schools in the sample covered all the content items prescribed for each level. They found that 82% of classes in the sample did not fully cover the mandatory minimum content (Contenidos Mínimos Obligatorios, CMOs) prescribed in the mathematics curriculum, and 74% did not cover all the CMOs of the language curriculum. The average of schools' overall curriculum coverage is between 50% and 60% of the CMOs of the level. This means that students may not acquire the learning associated with non-covered content and imples that teachers could use homework to make up for missed content.

- In **Poland**, the introduction of the new core curriculum in 2017 was accompanied by the phenomenon of assigning too much homework to primary school students. Teachers also spend a lot of time outside of school time preparing lesson plans and learning materials, fearing that they will not be able to complete all the teaching content of the core curriculum.

- **Kazakhstan** identifies homework overload as a particular consequence arising from teachers and students having to deal with an overloaded curriculum. Students are required to spend considerable time doing homework assigned by teachers in different subject areas (particularly in the compulsory subject areas), and this is having an impact on both personal life (sleep and leisure) and family life (weekends, vacations and meal times). In the 2016 national survey on students' experience with homework, almost half of students (48%) reported not finishing all their homework on time due to the heavy load. Almost half of the surveyed students (47%) in Grades 8 to 12 also reported that they wish that the amount of written homework could be reduced (Ministry of Education and Science of the Republic of Kazakhstan, 2016[6]).

Teacher overburden as a threat to teacher well-being

Curriculum overload is not synonymous with excessive workload for teachers, and many factors other than the curriculum have an impact on teacher workload. Nonetheless, when curriculum is overloaded and teachers feel pressure to cover all content, they may find themselves overburdened and spending time outside of working hours to meet expectations. Teachers who feel they have an unsustainable workload are more likely to experience burnout and more likely to leave the teaching profession (see "What does research say?"). In many countries and jurisdictions, ensuring that teacher well-being is not compromised as a result of teacher overburden is a key challenge for policy makers, as reported by Scotland (United Kingdom).

- Issues relating to teacher workload and perceptions of "bureaucracy in the curriculum" are a continuing challenge within **Scotland's (United Kingdom)** curriculum. The Scottish Government indicates that it continues to work with teaching unions to monitor workload and to consider how to address matters relating to workload in the system and that it is for local authorities and empowered head teachers to provide strong leadership at local level to ensure that curriculum development and delivery are manageable for teachers.

Curriculum pitch and workload: Strategies

As part of a comprehensive approach to curriculum redesign, many countries/jurisdictions are focusing not only on the structure of curriculum content, but also on regulating how the content should be delivered to students to meet their learning and well-being needs. This can be done by **regulating the learning time at school and at home** to allow for balance between learning activities and other activities that are equally essential for students' cognitive, social and emotional development.

Given that large paper-based curriculum documents can create a perception of overload, some countries/jurisdictions are **using digitalisation to address teacher overload**. Such an approach allows teachers to more easily navigate various through curriculum rubrics and interact with the curriculum in a more dynamic manner.

Regulating the learning time at school and at home

Countries/jurisdictions such as the Czech Republic, Finland and Kazakhstan, attempt to better align the instruction time in schools with the demands of curriculum. Such an approach aims to reduce pressure and overload on students by ensuring that sufficient time is given to acquire new competencies, while balancing this with requirements for students' well-being (e.g. resting and personal time, extra-curricular activities).

- The **Czech Republic** has attempted to ensure quality learning time by requiring curriculum designers to distribute time for formal education effectively among subject areas, taking into account the particular needs of communities and students.

- In its most recent curriculum reform, undertaken between 2014 and 2017, **Finland** set minimum lesson hours for national goals and key content areas and delegated authority to schools to make decisions on whether extra hours were required. The government set reduction of content in subject areas as a main goal, resulting in new core curriculum subject areas, including broader content areas, and the provision for local school authorities to select the actual content to be taught in each grade. In the new national core curriculum, subjects include broader content areas in three grade units (Grades 1-2, Grades 3-6 and Grades 7-9), from which local authorities choose the specific content to be taught in each grade.

- To address the issue of homework overload, **Kazakhstan's** Ministry of Education and Science presented two recommendations for public discussion on the organisation and implementation of homework in mainstream schools. The projects were proposed by two working groups, Nazarbayev Intellectual Schools and the Information and Analytical Center[1] under the Ministry of Education. Both projects are aimed at minimising the amount of homework and limiting the time spent on it by students from Grade 2 to Grade 11.

Using digitalisation to address teacher overload

Having a digitalised curriculum means teachers can easily navigate to the elements most relevant to their teaching practices, as reported by Australia. Such an approach means teachers do not have to wade through extraneous or irrelevant material in paper documents to reach what they need. This can lighten the load on teachers and reduce their perception of overload.

- The **Australian** Curriculum is published as an interactive digital curriculum. Teachers can access it from desktop computers, laptops, mobile devices or mobile phones in multiple views to best suit their needs. This strategy has also allowed teachers to filter the curriculum to customise the view for their particular purpose. For example, a school that wants to focus on developing the critical and creative thinking skills of its students can filter the curriculum by year/band, by subject and by the general capability of Critical and Creative Thinking.

- - - - -
Note

1. http://iac.kz/en/about-center.

References

Bempchat, J. (2004), "The motivational benefits of homework: A social-cognitive perspective", *Theory into Practice*, Vol. 43/3, pp. 189-196, http://dx.doi.org/10.1207/s15430421tip4303_4. [4]

Education Scotland (2016), *Curriculum for Excellence: A Statement for Practitioners from HM Chief Inspector of Education*, https://education.gov.scot/improvement/documents/cfestatement.pdf. [3]

Kim, K. et al. (2014), *문 이과 통합형 교육과정 총론 시안 개발 연구* [A study on the development of integrated curriculum of liberal arts and natural sciences: Initial draft.]. [2]

Kim, K. et al. (2015), *2015 개정 교육과정 총론 시안 [최종안] 개발 연구* [A study on the development of the national guidelines for the 2015 Revised Curriculum: Final draft.]. [1]

Marhefka, J. (2011), "Sleep deprivation: Consequences for students", *J Psychosoc Nurs Ment Health Serv.*, Vol. 49(9), pp. 20-25, http://dx.doi.org/10.3928/02793695-20110802-02. [5]

Ministry of Education and Science of the Republic of Kazakhstan (2016), *Organisation and Dosing of Homework of Kazakhstani students*, http://iac.kz/sites/default/files/proekt_1_-_prezentaciya-.pdf. [6]

What lessons have countries/ jurisdictions learned from unintended consequences?

The strategies introduced in the challenges and strategies section (see "What types of challenges do countries/jurisdictions face in addressing curriculum overload, and what strategies do they use to address these challenges?") could be options to address the challenges of managing curriculum overload. While the strategies may be helpful, they may also have unintended consequences. Some countries and jurisdictions have reported experiencing outcomes that were not anticipated when using these strategies. This added further complexity to minimising curriculum overload.

The following five key lessons learned are generated based on actual country experiences. These lessons can be used as a check list to reflect on the current state of play and avoid repeating similar unintended consequences that peer countries/jurisdictions have experienced.

Key lessons learned from unintended consequences on managing curriculum overload

- Keep the right balance between breadth of learning areas and depth of content knowledge.
- Use focus, rigour and coherence jointly as key design principles when addressing curriculum overload.
- Be conscious of and avoid homework overload for students.
- Be mindful of local decisions leading to curriculum overload for schools.
- Stress curriculum overload as a pressing issue by redefining student success and well-being.

---

1. KEEP THE RIGHT BALANCE BETWEEN BREADTH OF LEARNING AREAS AND DEPTH OF CONTENT KNOWLEDGE

How to ensure that both breadth of learning and depth of content knowledge are achievable within the allocated time in a curriculum remains a persistent dilemma for countries as they seek to prevent curriculum overload (See "What does research say?").

Altering selected content in the curriculum is politically challenging and a high-stakes undertaking. Curriculum change requires compromises and can result in the status quo for all content items if those compromises are not achieved. Changing content then often results in what is sometimes described as a "mile-wide-inch-deep" or shallow curriculum that does not allow students sufficient time to explore, understand and master the content. This can contribute to a sense of disengagement for students and teachers alike (See "What does research say?" and "What types of challenges do countries/jurisdictions face in addressing curriculum overload, and what strategies do they use to address these challenges?").

Countries/jurisdictions often face pressures to keep all content knowledge and learning hours in prioritised academic subjects, potentially at the expense of non-academic learning areas or content (See "What does research say?", "How do countries compare?"; and "What gets measured gets treasured" in (OECD, Forthcoming[1])). However, recent research findings suggest that non-academic subjects contribute not only to whole-child development, but also to students' cognitive and meta-cognitive development, which are considered key skills in academic subjects (concept note on skills[1] and e2030 PE report[2]).

Focusing solely on academic subjects may also disregard individual students' interests and strengths, as well as differences in their learning progression trajectories and the amount of time they may need to master content. To embrace such differentiation and diversity in a standardised document, some countries/jurisdictions have started to take a spiral curriculum approach, recognising non-linear learning progression and reinforcing material over time (See "What types of challenges do countries/jurisdictions face in addressing curriculum overload, and what strategies do they use to address these challenges?").

In sum, securing the breadth and depth of content learning is important, but securing the space and process built into curriculum redesign is equally important as they are interdependent. The depth of learning can be enhanced by focusing not only on student performance, but also on the quality of the student learning experinece as well as the quality of student-teacher interactions.

2. USE FOCUS, RIGOUR AND COHERENCE JOINTLY AS KEY DESIGN PRINCIPLES WHEN ADDRESSING CURRICULUM OVERLOAD

As design principles to guide curriculum development, focus suggests that a relatively small number of topics should be introduced to ensure deep, quality learning; rigour suggests that topics should be challenging and enable deep thinking and reflection, which is not to be confused with rigid or inflexible design; and coherence suggests that topics should be ordered in a logical way to create a progression (OECD, 2019[2]). Each of the principles has its own challenges for implementation. But, they should be used jointly to avoid unintended consequences of using them one by one.

When reducing content, focusing on a relatively small number of topics can be met not only with resistance from stakeholders defending their subjects and interests, but also with a perception of lowering the quality and standards of education. This could, in turn, result in a backlash from key stakeholders that might lead to increased content and instruction time in subsequent reforms (See "What does research say?" and "What types of challenges do countries/jurisdictions face in addressing curriculum overload, and what strategies do they use to address these challenges?").

It is, therefore, critical to strike **the right balance between focus and rigour**, articulating the importance of rigour to key stakeholders when focusing on core elements or selected concepts, contents and big ideas. At the same time, excess remains the enemy. Countries/jurisdictions reported that an overly rigorous curriculum may put students of disadvantaged backgrounds more at risk of falling behind and dropping out and may also lead to teachers not being able to cover all content during the allotted instruction time (See "3. Be aware of homework overload for students"). Thus, a balance of rigour and focus may help to ensure that all students are able to access and engage with the material.

To achieve a well-balanced curriculum, **coherence** is also essential. It is critical to ensure that topics are not removed without due regard to maintaining the logic and the appropriate sequential learning that exists in each discipline. This should be done while avoiding unnecessary overlap and/or duplication across grades and across subjects (See "What does research say?" and "What types of challenges do countries/jurisdictions face in addressing curriculum overload, and what strategies do they use to address these challenges?"). To make this happen, it is essential to engage subject experts (academics and practitioners) in cross-subject co-ordination from the onset of a curriculum reform process. They can undertake their drafting tasks within set boundaries without compromising the integrity and logic of individual disciplines/subject areas.

A coherent curriculum can also support articulating how certain topics can be related across different disciplines, suggesting possible ways to promote interdisciplinary learning. It ensures that the specified standards are pitched at developmentally appropriate levels (grade and age), while supporting teachers to respond to learners' needs where student learning progress is framed by broader purposes. By adding focus, rigour and coherence combined into the curriculum redesign process, policy makers could therefore aim for a well-balanced curriculum in order to mitigate further overload.

3. BE CONSCIOUS OF AND AVOID HOMEWORK OVERLOAD FOR STUDENTS

When teachers are not able to cover the intended content within the allocated instruction time, they are likely to leave it up to students to catch up on the content on their own, resulting in homework overload. This was highlighted as a pressing issue by the students' group of the OECD Future of Education and Skills project, in particular, with online learning or hybrid model as experience in the context of COVID-19 in 2020.

Excessive homework in turn has repercussions on after-school hours, leaving less time to sleep, play, eat and spend time with friends and family, with an ultimately negative impact on students' health and well-being (See "What does research say?" and "What types of challenges do countries/jurisdictions face in addressing curriculum overload, and what strategies do they use to address these challenges?"). In addition, out-of-school work can increase teachers' workload for homework preparation and marking. In short, homework overload can adversely influence both students and teachers.

Quality and complexity of homework are key components to keep in mind when mitigating homework overload. Homework is increasingly associated with new pedagogies (such as flipped classrooms or project-based learning), which require more complex assignments to be taken at home. If homework becomes too complex, students are more likely to become disengaged. A possible unintended consequence is the disproportionate effect on disadvantaged students (OECD, Forthcoming[3]), who may not be able to rely on the same support at home as advantaged students. It may thus have repercussions on perceptions/experience of overload, disengagement and possibly dropout rates.

However, a balance needs to be struck between complex and oversimplified homework. Some countries/jurisdictions have reported that simple tasks or drills (e.g. in mathematics or via digital platforms) might contribute to demotivation and disengagement among students (OECD, Forthcoming[3]).While these types of tasks are easier for teachers to assign and assess and thus decrease overload in the short term, they may lead to more work and increased overload in the longer term.

When designed well, homework can also be beneficial for students, such as for long-term development of children's motivation, strategies for coping with mistakes and setbacks and the time for children to develop positive beliefs about achievement (Bempchat, 2004[4]). Therefore, it is important that, before giving homework, teachers should ask themselves what kinds of homework is appropriate for diverse learners, so that the materials would help avoid excessive work for teachers and that students would not have undue pressures beyond the school day.

4. BE MINDFUL OF LOCAL DECISIONS LEADING TO CURRICULUM OVERLOAD FOR SCHOOLS

Schools and teachers are increasingly given responsibility in curriculum management in countries/jurisdictions where curriculum adaptations or autonomy are granted at the local or school level, to ensure that the curriculum meets the needs of students and of local communities.

However, some countries/jurisdictions report that curriculum overload tends to be heavier at the local level, with teachers and schools overburdened by the responsibilities such autonomy entails. This could be due to a lack of guidance on what to remove or what to prioritise in curriculum content at the school and local levels (See "What types of challenges do countries/jurisdictions face in addressing curriculum overload, and what strategies do they use to address these challenges?"). But it could also be due, as some countries/jurisdictions have experienced, to guidelines that are too prescriptive (e.g. teachers teaching the examples word for word). Teachers may also find it difficult to combine new competencies and subjects with traditional ones, contributing to an even greater perception of overload and a decreased sense of self-efficacy and motivation to teach.

It is, therefore, of critical importance to ensure proper initial teacher training and to offer guidance, continuous training and materials to accompany teachers and school leaders through the process of curriculum redesign and implementation. Such an intentional process of guidance and training can help ensure autonomy and lead to more efficiency rather than more overload (See "What does research say?").

In fact, much of the success of curricular redesign depends on the culture in which teachers and school leaders are operating. If teachers are encouraged to have agency, to be the designers, co-creators and facilitators of the curriculum and are properly equipped, they will find themselves making room for the intended goals of the curriculum that are relevant for their students' future.

5. STRESS CURRICULUM OVERLOAD AS A PRESSING ISSUE BY REDEFINING STUDENT SUCCESS AND WELL-BEING

When a curriculum reform is undertaken, the goals of education and the nature of the learner and/or the vision for young learners are often revisited. All stakeholders – policy makers, teachers and school leaders, academics and parents – strive for student success. This includes not only academic success, but also success in life as healthy, active and responsible citizens. The goals of education recognise the importance of students' well-being which, as previously noted, also means enough time to sleep, to play with friends, to eat and to spend time with the family (See "What does research say?").

However, well-intended goals regarding student well-being can be undermined if there is not enough space in the curriculum, and there are often pressures to retain and even add material within curricula. Subject experts, such as school teachers or faculty members, can often defend the retention of favoured content and press for their expansion (See "What types of challenges do countries/jurisdictions face in addressing curriculum overload, and what strategies do they use to address these challenges?"). Special interest groups can perceive the reduction/removal of subject content as a threat to their job security, which may promote an adherence to teaching and learning within rigid subject area boundaries, rather than utilising opportunities to use integrated approaches to enhance, and deepen students' overall learning. Content tribalism, as this is sometimes called, can thus pose obstacles to efforts to reduce curriculum content and promote transdisciplinary approaches.

When confronted with difficulties in reaching consensus, reconciling tensions and contradictory views from a wide range of stakeholders, it is important to remind everyone of the intended ultimate beneficiaries of the curriculum redesign – the students and their holistic development (see "Lessons learned" section in (OECD, Forthcoming[1])). In doing so, actively bringing in the voice of students, allowing them to participate in the planning of curriculum content, raising concerns and presenting ideas on how their learning and ultimately well-being can be improved, would be an important step forward (see "Lessons learned on student voice, choice and agency" in (OECD, Forthcoming[5])).

By moving away from the notion of "more is better", student success can be rethought and redefined to embrace student well-being and to put it at the centre of curriculum reform and education overall. Such a redefinition would lead to cultural change in society and hence a change in priorities for stakeholders, recognising that an appropriately balanced curriculum is best for the well-being of students.

- - - - - -

Notes

1. http://www.oecd.org/education/2030-project/teaching-and-learning/learning/skills/Skills_for_2030_concept_note.pdf

2. https://www.oecd.org/education/2030-project/contact/OECD_FUTURE_OF_EDUCATION_2030_MAKING_PHYSICAL_DYNAMIC_AND_INCLUSIVE_FOR_2030.pdf

References

Bempchat, J. (2004), "The motivational benefits of homework: A social-cognitive perspective", *Theory into Practice*, Vol. 43/3, pp. 189-196, http://dx.doi.org/10.1207/s15430421tip4303_4. [4]

OECD (2020), *What Students Learn Matters: Towards a 21st Century Curriculum*, OECD Publishing, Paris, https://doi.org/10.1787/d86d4d9a-en. [2]

OECD (Forthcoming), *An Ecosystem Approach to Curriculum Redesign and Implementation* (working title), OECD Publishing, Paris. [1]

OECD (Forthcoming), *Curriculum Flexibility and Autonomy* (working title), OECD Publishing, Paris. [5]

OECD (Forthcoming), *Equity Through Curriculum Innovations* (working title), OECD Publishing, Paris. [3]

Contributors list

NATIONAL CO-ORDINATORS FROM OECD COUNTRIES AND JURISDICTIONS FOR THE OECD FUTURE OF EDUCATION AND SKILLS 2030 PROJECT

Australia: Danielle Cavanagh (Australian Curriculum Assessment and Reporting Authority (ACARA)), Patrick Donaldson (Permanent Delegation of Australia to the OECD), Janet Davy (ACARA), Hilary Dixon (ACARA), Mark McAndrew (ACARA), Fiona Mueller (ACARA), Robert Randall (ACARA)

Belgium: Dominique Denis (Ministère de la Fédération Wallonie-Bruxelles) Marie-Anne Persoons (Flemish Department of Education and Training), Kirsten Bulteen (Flemish Community of Belgium)

Canada: Council of Ministers of Education Canada - CMEC: Marianne Roaldi; Marie Macauley; Marie-France Chouinard (Délégation permanente du Canada auprès de l'OCDE); **Ontario**: Richard Franz (Ontario Ministry of Education), Angela Hinton (Ontario Ministry of Education), Cathy Montreuil (Ontario Ministry of Education), Shirley Kendrick (Ontario Ministry of Education), Safa Zaki (Ontario Ministry of Education), Lori Stryker (Ontario Ministry of Education), Cresencia Fong (Ontario Ministry of Education); **Québec**: Geneviève LeBlanc (Ministère de l'Éducation et de l'Enseignement supérieur), Marie-Ève Laviolette (Ministère de l'Éducation et de l'Enseignement supérieur), Julie-Madeleine Roy (Ministère de l'Éducation et de l'Enseignement supérieur), Andrée Racine (Ministère de l'Éducation et de l'Enseignement supérieur); **Manitoba**: Carolee Buckler (Manitoba Education and Advanced Learning), Dallas Morrow (Manitoba Department of Education and Training); **British Columbia**: Keith Godin (Ministry of Education of British Columbia), Angie Calleberg (Ministry of Education of British Columbia), Nick Poeschek (Ministry of Education of British Columbia), Nancy Walt (Ministry of Education of British Columbia); **Saskatchewan**: Susan Nedelcov-Anderson (Ministry of Education of Saskatchewan)

Chile: Eliana Chamizo Álvarez (Ministry of Education), Francisca Müller (Permanent Delegation of Chile to the OECD) Ana Labra Welden (Ministry of Education), Alejandra Arratia Martínez (Ministry of Education)

Czech Republic: Hana Novotná (Minsitry of Education)

Denmark: Rasmus Biering-Sorensen (Danish Ministry of Education), Jens Rasmussen (Aarhus University), Christian Lamhauge Rasmussen (Danish Ministry of Education), Pernille Skou Bronner Andersen (Danish Ministry of Education)

Estonia: Heli Aru-Chabilan (Ministry of Education and Research), Imbi Henno (Ministry of Education and Research), Eve Kikas (Tallinn University), Maie Kitsing (Ministry of Education and Research), Pille Liblik (Ministry of Education and Research), Kärt-Katrin Pere (Foundation Innove), Katrin Rein (Permanent Representation of Estonia to the OECD and UNESCO

Finland: Aleksi Kalenius (Permanent Delegation of Finland to the OECD), Aki Tornberg (Ministry of Education and Culture), Anneli Rautiainen (Finnish National Agency for Education), Erja Vitikka (Finnish National Agency for Education)

France: Claudio Cimelli (Ministère de l'Education Nationale), Mireille Lamouroux (Ministère de l'Education Nationale), Pascale Montrol-Amouroux (Ministère de l'Education Nationale), Daniel Schlosser (Permanent Delegation of France to the OECD)

Germany: Jutta Illichmann (Bundesministerium für Bildung und Forschung) Elfriede Ohrnberger (Bayerisches Staatsministerium für Bildung und Kultus, Wissenschaft und Kunst), Birgitta Ryberg (Secretariat of the Standing Conference of the Ministers of Education and Cultural Affairs of the Laender in the Federal Republic of Germany)

Greece: Katerina Zizel Kantali (Permanent Delegation of Greece to the OECD), Aikaterini Trimi Kyrou (Ministry of National Education and Religious Affairs)

Hungary: Andras Hlacs (Permanent Delegation of Hungary to the OECD), László Limbacher (Ministry of Human Capacities), Nora Katona (Eszterházy Károly Egyetem O2030), Valéria Csépe (MTA RCNS Brain Imaging Centre & Eszterházy Károly Egyetem O2030)

Iceland: Ásgerdur Kjartansdóttir (Ministry of Education, Science and Culture), Ásta Magnusdottir (Ministry of Education, Science and Culture)

Ireland: Suzanne Dillon (Department of Education and Skills), Breda Naughton (Department of Education and Skills), Linda Neary (Department of Education and Skills)

Israel: Sivan Kfir Katz (Permanent Delegation of Israel to the OECD), Meirav Zarviv (Israeli Ministry of Education)

Italy: Donatella Solda Kutzmann (Ministry of Education)

Japan: Jun Aoki (Ministry of Education, Culture, Sports, Science and Technology (MEXT)) Kazuo Akiyama (MEXT), Hajime Furusaka (MEXT), Eri Hata (MEXT), Taka Horio (MEXT), Hiroshi Itakura (MEXT), Tetsuya Kashihara (Permanent Delegation of Japan to the OECD), Takashi Kiryu (Permanent Delegation of Japan to the OECD), Hideaki Matsugi (MEXT), Yuiko Minami (MEXT), Takashi Murao (Permanent Delegation of Japan to the OECD), Ayaka Masuda (MEXT), Kana Setoguchi (MEXT), Shun Shirai (MEXT), Kan Hiroshi Suzuki (The Univercity of Tokyo), Taijiro Tsuruoka (MEXT), Daiki Ujishi (MEXT)

Korea: Moonhee Kim (Permanent Delegation of the Republic of Korea to the OECD), Hyunjin Kim (Permanent Delegation of Korea to the OECD), Jong-Won Yoon (Permanent Delegation of the Republic of Korea to the OECD), Mee-Kyeong Lee (Korea Institute for Curriculum and Evaluation), Keun Ho Lee (Korea Institute for Curriculum and Evaluation), Sangeun Lee (Korean Education Development Institutes), Keejoon Yoon (Incheon National University), Hee-Hyun Byun (Korea Institute for Curriculum and Evaluation), Keun-ho Lee (Korea Institute for Curriculum and Evaluation), Su-Jin Choi (Korean Educational Development Institute), Haemee Rim (Korea Institute for Curriculum and Evaluation)

Latvia: Laura Treimane (Permanent Delegation of the Republic of Latvia to the OECD and UNESCO) Guntars Catlaks (National Education Centre), Jelena Muhina (Ministry of Education and Science), Zane Olina (Competency Based Curriculum Project, National Centre for Education)

Lithuania: Šarūnė Nagrockaitė (Vilnius University), Irena Raudiene (Ministry of Education and Science)

Luxembourg: Michel Lanners (Ministère de l'Éducation nationale, de l'Enfance et de la Jeunesse)

Mexico: Carla Musi (Permanent Delegation of Mexico to the OECD), Elisa Bonilla Rius (Secretaría de Educación Pública), Carlos Tena (Permanent Delegation of Mexico to the OECD)

Netherlands: Marjolijn de Boer (Ministry of Education Culture and Science), Willem Rosier (Netherlands institute for curriculum development) Jeanne van Loon (Dutch Ministry of Education, Culture and Science), Jeroen Postma (Ministry of Education Culture and Science), Marc Van Zanten (Netherlands institute for curriculum development), Berend Brouwer (Netherlands institute for curriculum development)

New Zealand: Chris Arcus (Ministry of Education), Shelley Robertson (Ministry of Education), Gracielli Ghizzi-Hall (Ministry of Education), Pauline Cleaver (Ministry of Education), Denise Arnerich (Curriculum Design & Assessment)

Norway: Elisabeth Buk-Berge (Ministry of Education and Research), Reidunn Aarre Matthiessen (Norwegian Directorate for Education and Training), Bente Heian (Norwegian Directorate for Education and Training), Siv Hilde Lindstrom (Permanent Delegation of Norway to the OECD and UNESCO)

Poland: Rafal Lew-Starowicz (Ministry of National Education), Danuta Pusek (Ministry of National Education), Witold Zakrzewski (Ministry of National Education)

Portugal: Eulália Alexandre (Ministry of Education), Duarte Bue Alves (Permanent Delegation of Portugal to the OECD) João Costa (Ministry of Education) Ines Goncalves (Permanent Delegation of Portugal to the OECD) Elma Pereira (Permanent Delegation of Portugal to the OECD), Luisa Ucha-Silva (Ministry of Education)

Spain: Carmen Tovar Sanchez (Ministry of Education, Culture and Sport), Jaime Vaquero (Ministry of Education, Culture and Sport), María Saladich (Délégations Permanentes de l'Espagne auprès de l'OCDE, l'UNESCO et le Conseil de l'Europe)

Sweden: Anna Westerholm (Swedish National Agency for Education), Katalin Bellaagh (Swedish National Agency for Education), Johan Börjesson (Swedish National Agency for Education), Ann-Christin Hartman (Swedish National Agency for Education), Helena Karis (Swedish National Agency for Education), Jenny Lindblom (Swedish National Agency for Education)

United Kingdom, Scotland: Joan Mackay (Education Scotland), Elaine Kelley (Scottish Government), Judith Tracey (Scottish Government), Kit Wyeth (Scottish Government), Jonathan Wright (Scottish Government); **Wales**: Steve Davies (Education and Public Service Group), Kevin Mark Palmer (Education Achievement Service for South East Wales) Debbie Lewis (Central South Consortium, Wales), Ruth Thackray (GwE Representing Welsh Government)

United States: Mary Coleman (U.S. Department of Education)

NATIONAL CO-ORDINATORS FROM PARTNER COUNTRIES AND ECONOMIES FOR THE OECD FUTURE OF EDUCATION AND SKILLS 2030 PROJECT

Argentina: Inés Cruzalegui (Ministerio de Educatión Nacional), Mercedes Miguel (Ministerio de Educatión Nacional)

China (People's Republic of): Huisheng Tian (National Center for School Curriculum and Textbook Development, Ministry of Education of China), Yangnan Wang (National Center for Education Development Research), Haixia Xu (National Center for Education Development Research)

Costa Rica: Alicia Vargas (Ministerio de Educación Pública), Rosa Carranza (Ministerio de Educación Pública)

Hong Kong (China): Chi-kong Chau (Education Bureau), Joe Ka-shing Ng (Education Bureau), Ashley Pak-wai Leung (Education Bureau), Winnie Wing-man Leung (Education Bureau), Henry Ting-kit Lin (Education Bureau)Vincent Siu-chuen Chan (Education Bureau), Annie Hing-yee Wong (Education Bureau)

Indonesia: Taufik Hanafi (Ministry of Education and Culture

Kazakhstan: Zhanar Abdildina (Nazarbayev Intellectual Schools AEO), Yeldos Nurlanov (JSC Information-Analytical Center), Aizhan Ramazanova (Nazarbayev Intellectual Schools AEO), Dina Shaikhina (Nazarbayev Intellectual Schools AEO), Azhar Kabdulinova (Nazarbayev Intellectual Schools AEO), Nazipa Ayubayeva (Nazarbayev Intellectual Schools AEO)

Lebanon: Rana Abdallah (Center for Educational Research and Development)

Russian Federation: Kirill Bykov (Ambassade de Russie en France), Maria Dobryakova (National Research University Higher School of Economics), Isak Froumin (National Research University Higher School of Economics), Anastasia Sviridova (Far Eastern Federal University) Elena Minina (Institute of Education HSE) Elizaveta Pozdniakova (Federal Institute for the Evaluation of Quality education), Sergey Stanchenko (Federal Institute for the Evaluation of the Education Quality), Shivleta Tagirova (Ministry of Education and Science - MEC)

Saudi Arabia: Nayyaf Aljabri (Ministry of Education), Lama Al-Qarawi (Ministery of Education), Meetb Al-Humaidan (Ministery of Education), Abdulrahman Alsayari (Ministery of Education), Hissah Bin-Zuayer (Ministery of Education)

Singapore: Oon Seng Tan (National Institute of Education, Nanyang Technological University), Low Ee Ling (National Institute of Education, Nanyang Technological University), Lim Kek Joo (National Institute of Education, Nanyang Technological University),

Slovenia: Ksenija Bregar-Golobic (Ministry of Education, Science and Sport)

South Africa: SP Govender (Minstry of Education) and H Mabunda (Ministry of Education)

United Arab Emirates: Tareq Mana S. Al Otaiba (Abu Dhabi Crown Prince Court)

Viet Nam: Tran Cong Phong (Vietnam Institute of Educational Sciences), Do Duc Lan (Vietnam Institute of Educational Sciences), Anh Nguyen Ngoc (Vietnam Institute of Educational Sciences), Luong Viet Thai (Vietnam Institute of Educational Sciences), Le Anh Vinh (Vietnam Institute of Educational Sciences)

NATIONAL CO-ORDINATORS AND CONTACT PERSONS FOR THE POLICY QUESTIONNAIRE ON CURRICULUM REDESIGN (PQC)

Australia: Hilary Dixon (Australian Curriculum Assessment and Reporting Authority (ACARA)), Robert Randall (ACARA)

Argentina: Mercedes Miguel (Ministerio de Educatión Nacional)

Canada, British Columbia: Angie Calleberg (British Columbia, Ministry of Education), Nick Poeschek (British Columbia, Ministry of Education) and Nancy Walt (British Columbia, Ministry of Education); **Ontario**: Martyn Beckett, (Ontario Ministry of Education), Shirley Kendrick (Ontario Ministry of Education), Cathy Montreuil (Ontario Ministry of Education), Yael Ginsler (Ontario Ministry of Education); **Québec**: Geneviève LeBlanc (Ministère de l'Éducation et de l'Enseignement supérieur), Marie-Ève Laviolette (Ministère de l'Éducation et de l'Enseignement supérieur)

Chile: María Jesús Honorato (Ministry of Education) and Ruth Cortez (Ministry of Education)

China (People's Republic of): Huisheng Tian (National Institute of Education Sciences), Yan Wang (National Institute of Education Sciences)

Costa Rica: Rosa Carranza (Ministerio de Educación Pública), Alicia Vargas (Ministerio de Educación Pública)

Czech Republic: Hana Novotna (Czech School Inspectorate)

Denmark: Christian Rasmussen (Ministry of Education), Pernille Skou Bronner Andersen (Ministry of Education)

Estonia: Pille Liblik (Ministry of Education and Research), Imbi Henno (Ministry of Education and Research)

Finland: Aki Tornberg (Ministry of Education and Culture), Erja Vitikka (Finnish National Agency for Education)

Hong Kong (China): Joe Ka-shing Ng (Education Bureau)

Hungary: Valeria Csepe (Eszterházy Károly University), Nora Katona (Eszterházy Károly University)

Ireland: Linda Neary (Department of Education and Skills)

Japan: Takanori Bando (Ministry of Education, Culture, Sports, Science and Technology (MEXT)), Hiroshi Itakura (MEXT), Yoichi Kiyohara (MEXT), Shun Shirai (MEXT), Kouchiro Tatsumi (National Institute for Educational Policy Research), Aya Yamamoto (MEXT)

Kazakhstan: Zhanar Abdildina (Nazarbayev Intellectual Schools AEO), Dina Shaikhina (Nazarbayev Intellectual Schools AEO)

Korea: Mee-Kyeong Lee (Korea Institute for Curriculum and Evaluation), Eun Young Kim (Korean Educational Development Institute)

Mexico: Elisa Bonilla Rius (Secretaría de Educación Pública)

Netherlands: Jeanne van Loon (Dutch Ministry of Education, Culture and Science)

New Zealand: Pauline Cleaver (Ministry of Education), Gracielli Ghizzi-Hall (Ministry of Education)

Norway: Elisabeth Buk-Berge (Ministry of Education and Research), Bente Heian (Norwegian Directorate for Education and Training)

Poland: Danuta Pusek (Ministry of National Education)

Portugal: Eulália Alexandre (Ministry of Education)

Russian Federation: Maria Dobryakova (National Research University Higher School of Economics), Tatiana Meshkova (National Research University Higher School of Economics), Elena Sabelnikova (National Research University Higher School of Economics)

Singapore: Low Ee Ling (National Institute of Education, Nanyang Technological University)

South Africa: Suren Govender (Department of Basic Education), Hleki Mabunda (Department of Basic Education)

Sweden: Johan Börjesson (Swedish National Agency for Education)

United Kingdom, Scotland: Jonathan Wright (Education Analysis); **Wales**: Rhiannon Davies (Education and Public Services Group)

Viet Nam: Luong Viet Thai (Vietnam Institute of Education Sciences)

Researchers contributing to the Policy Questionnaire on Curriculum Resign (PQC) for their countries:

Brazil: Claudia Costin (Center for Innovation and Excellence in Educational Policies), Allan Michel Jales Coutinho (Center for Innovation and Excellence in Educational Policies)

India: Monal Jayaram Poduval (Piramal Foundation for Education Leadership), Lopa Gandhi (Gandhi Fellowship), Shrestha Ganguly (Piramal Foundation for Education Leadership), Shobhana Panikar (Kaivalya Education Foundation)

United Kingdom, Northern Ireland: Carmel Gallagher (International Bureau for Education)

United States: William Schmidt (Michigan State University), Leland Cogan (Michigan State University), Jennifer Cady (Michigan State University)

NATIONAL EXPERTS FOR CURRICULUM CONTENT MAPPING (CCM)

Australia: Hilary Dixon (Australian Curriculum Assessment and Reporting Authority (ACARA)), Mark McAndrew (ACARA), Danielle Cavanagh (ACARA), Julie King (ACARA), Kim Reid (ACARA), Rainer Mittelbach (ACARA), Nancy Incoll (ACARA), Amanda Green (ACARA)

Canada: Marie Macauley (Council of Ministers of Education of Canada (CMEC)), Katerina Sukovski (CMEC), Antonella Manca-Mangoff (CMEC), Marie-France Chouinard (CMEC); **Ontario**: Cathy Montreuil (Ontario Ministry of Education), Shawna Eby (Ontario Ministry of Education), Whitney Philippi (Ontario Ministry of Education), Shirley Kendrick (Ontario Ministry of Education), Saeeda Foss (Ontario Ministry of Education), Dianne Oliphant (Ontario Ministry of Education), Yael Ginsler (Ontario Ministry of Education); **British Columbia**: Angie Calleberg, Nancy Walt (British Columbia Ministry of Education); **Saskatchewan**: Susan Nedelcov-Anderson (Council of Ministers of Education of Canada, CMEC)

Chile: Ana Labra Welden (Ministry of Education), María Elena Ponton Caceres (Ministry of Education), Alejandra Arratia Martínez (Ministry of Education)

Czech Republic: Hana Novotná (Czech School Inspectorate), Petr Koubek (National Institute for Education), Daniel Mares (National Institute for Education)

Denmark: Pernille Skou Brønner Andersen (Ministry of Education)

Estonia: Imbi Henno (Ministry of Education and Research), Hele Liiv-Tellmann (Curriculum and Methodology Agency, Foundation Innove), Pille Liblik (Ministry of Education and Research)

Finland: Aki Tornberg (Ministy of Education), Anneli Rautiainen (Finnish National Agency for Education), Erja Vitikka (Finnish National Agency for Education)

Greece: Vasiliki Sakka (Ministry of Education, Research and Religious Affairs)

Israel: Gilmor Keshet-Maor (Ministry of Education)

Ireland: Suzanne Dillon (Department of Education and Skills), Linda Neary (Department of Education and Skills)

Japan: Kazuo Akiyama (Ministry of Education, Culture, Sports, Science and Technology, (MEXT)), Takashi Asakura (Tokyo Gakugei University), Takanori Bando (MEXT), Takashi Kiryu (Permanent Delegation of Japan to the OECD), Yoichi Kiyohara (MEXT), Tadashi Otani (Tokyo Gakugei University), Shun Shirai (MEXT), Mihoko Toyoshima (MEXT)

Korea: Jong-Yun Kim (Korea Institute for Curriculum and Evaluation), Mee-Kyeong Lee (Korea Institute for Curriculum and Evaluation), Jiyoung Seo (Korea Institute for Curriculum and Evaluation), Keejoon Yoon (Incheon National University), Keun-ho Lee (Korea Institute for Curriculum and Evaluation), Ki-Chul Kim (Korea Institute for Curriculum and Evaluation), Chang-Wan Yu (Incheon National University), Jaejin Lee (Korea Institute for Curriculum and Evaluation)

Lithuania: Zita Nauckunaite (Education Development Centre), Irena Raudiene (Ministry of Education and Science), Šarūnė Nagrockaitė (Faculty of Philosophy, Vilnius University).

Netherlands: Annette Thijs (Curriculum Expert), Bart Penning de Vries (Curriculum Expert, humanities), Frederik Oorschot (Curriculum Expert, humanities), Marc van Zanten (Curriculum Expert, mathematics), Suzanne Sjoers (Curriculum Expert, mathematics), Allard Strijker (Curriculum Expert, digital literacy), Jos Tolboom, digital literacy), Erik Woldhuis (Curriculum Expert, science), Jeroen Sijbers(Curriculum Expert, science).

Norway: Elisabeth Buk-Berge (Ministry of Education and Research)

Portugal: Eulália Alexandre (Directorate General for Education), Carla Mota (Directorate General for Education), Helena Peralta (University of Lisbon), Sónia Valente Rodrigues (University of Porto), Maria do Céu Roldão (Portuguese Catholic University, Lisbon), Joana Viana (University of Lisbon)

Poland: Jerzy Wisniewski (Curriculum Expert)

Slovakia: Vladislav Ujhazi (Permanent Delegation of the Slovak Republic to the OECD), Alena Minns (Slovak Youth Institute)

Sweden: Anna Karin Frisk (Swedish National Agency for Education), Helena Karis (Swedish National Agency for Education), Johan Börjesson (Swedish National Agency for Education)

United Kingdom, Northern Ireland: Roisin Radcliffe (Council for the Curriculum, Examinations and Assessment)

United States: Hector Brown (Permanent Delegation of the United States to the OECD)

India: Monal Jayaram (Piramal Foundation for Education Leadership), Anshu Dubey (Piramal Foundation for Education Leadership)

Kazakhstan: Dina Shaikhina (Center for Educational Programmes)

Latvia: Zane Olina (National Centre for Education)

Lebanon: Rana Abdallah (Curriculum Expert)

China (People's Republic of): Huisheng Tian (National Center for School Curriculum and Textbook Development, NCCT), Yuexia Liu (National Center for School Curriculum and Textbook Development, NCCT), Hongwei Meng (PESAI Research Institute), Hua Guo (Beijing Normal University), Lijie Lv (Northeast Normal University), Kit Tai Hau (The Chinese University of Hong Kong), Jiayong Li (Beijing Normal University), Zaiping Zeng (PESAI Research Institute), Yongjun Liu (SRT Education), Jianying Ren (NCCT), Yunfeng Wang (Capital Normal University), Guihua Zheng (Shanghai Normal University), Qinli Gao (SRT Education), Yunpeng Ma (Northeast Normal University), Yiming Cao (Beijing Normal University), Jianyue Zhang (SRT Education), Boqin Liao (Southwest University), Bing Liu (Tsinghua University), Lei Wang (Beijing Normal University), Changlong Zheng (Northeast Normal University), Jian Wang (Beijing Normal University), Lixiang Zhu (SRT Education), Yuying Guo (Beijing Normal University), Jiemin Liu (Beijing Normal University), Guoliang Yu (Renmin University of China), Jun He (SRT Education), Peiying Lin (Capital Normal University), Min Wang (Beijing Normal University), Lin Zheng (Beijing Normal University), Pei Liu (China Conservatory of Music), Zhifan Hu (Shanghai Normal University), Shaochun Yin (Capital Normal University), Jin Song (Central Conservatory of Music), Xiaozan Wang (East China Normal University), Shaowei Pan (Yangzhou University), Xinrui Feng (National Institute of Education Sciences), Zhong Lin (People's Education Press), Yunlong Chen (NCCT), Shanshan Wang (NCCT), Na Wei (NCCT), Lixia Zhao (NCCT), Ying Liu (NCCT) Ying Yi (NCCT)

Russian Federation: Maria Dobryakova (National Research University Higher School of Economics), Isak Frumin (National Research University - Higher School of Economics).

Singapore: Ee Ling Low (National Institute of Education)

Viet Nam: Anh Nguyen Ngoc (Vietnam Institute of Educational Sciences), Do Duc Lan (Vietnam Institute of Educational Sciences), Luong Viet Thai (Vietnam Institute of Educational Sciences)

MEMBERS OF THE EDUCATION POLICY COMMITTEE/ EDUCATION COUNSELLORS

Members of the OECD's Education Policy Committee and education counsellors also provided valuable contributions by making relevant interventions during the discussions at the Committee meetings and/ or by reviewing the draft report prior to publication.

CURRICULUM EXPERTS

Roderick Allen (Superintendent, Saint George), Richard Bailey (Richard Bailey Education and Sport Ltd, United Kingdom), Marius R. Busemeyer (University of Konstanz, Germany), Leland Cogan (Michigan State University, United States), Jere Confrey (North Carolina State University, United States), Lianghuo Fan (East China Normal University, China), Jennifer Groff (MIT Media Lab, United States), Anna Gromada (Institut de Recherche et Documentation en Economie de la Santé, France), Irmeli Halinen (Metodix Oy (Ltd), Finland), Phil Lambert (Phil Lambert Consulting, Australia), Elena Minina (Higher School of Economics, Russia),

William Schmidt (Michigan State University, United States), Kimberly Schonert-Reichl (University of British Columbia), Claire Sinnema (University of Auckland, New Zealand), Jan van den Akker (Curriculum Research & Consultancy, Netherlands), Joke Voogt (University of Amsterdam and Windesheim University, Netherlands), Louise Zarmati (University of Tasmania, Australia), Liat Zwirn (Concept, Israel)

STUDENT CONTRIBUTORS

Maria Cardia (Student, Agrupamento de Escolas Moimenta da Beira, Portugal), Jay Hamidova (Student, Gleneagle Secondary School, British Columbia, Canada), Ayumi Mitsui (Student, Toshimagaoka Joshi Gakuen Junior & Senior High School, Japan)

OECD SECRETARIAT

Management group

Andreas Schleicher (Director for Education and Skills), Dirk Van Damme (Senior Counsellor), Yuri Belfali (Head of Division)

OECD Future of Education and Skills 2030 team

Project manager, Senior analyst: Miho Taguma, **Analysts:** Esther Carvalhaes, Meritxell Fernández Barrera, Alena Frid, Lauren Kavanagh, Natalie Laechelt, Fumitaka Suzuki, **Assistants:** Kevin Gillespie, Leslie Greenhow, Hanna Varkki, **Consultants:** Joaquin Carceles Martinez, Tamara Evdokimova, Kelly Makowiecki, **Thomas J. Alexander Fellow:** Sara Anderson, **Editor:** Susan Copeland, **Design:** Sophie Limoges, Della Shin

OECD former Secretariat members

Analysts: Eva Feron, Misuk Kim, Masafumi Ishikawa, Soumaya Maghnouj, Nathan Roberson, Shun Shirai, Kristina Sonmark, Makito Yurita, **Statistician:** Manon Costinot, **Consultants:** Alison Burke, Connie Chung, Najung Kim, Meow Hwee Lim, Yubai Wu, **Assistant:** Carrie Richardson, **Intern:** Yeasong Kim

Expert reviewers

Tadahiko Abiko (Distinguished Invited Professor, Kanagawa University, Professor Emeritus, Nagoya University), Kiyomi Akita (Dean, Graduate School of Education, The University of Tokyo), Stephan Vincent-Lancrin (Senior Analyst, OECD), Mathias Bouckaert (Analyst, OECD), Phil Lambert (Phil Lambert Consulting, Australia), Tim Oates (Cambridge Assessment, United Kingdom)